Special Educational Needs: Towards a Whole School Approach

Mel Ainscow and Anton Florek (Eds.)

David Fulton Publishers
and
National Council for Special Education

David Fulton Publishers Ltd
2 Barbon Close, Great Ormond Street, London WC1N 3JX

First published in Great Britain by
David Fulton Publishers 1989,
in association with National Council for Special Education

British Library Cataloguing in Publication Data

Special educational needs: towards a whole school approach
  1. Special education
  I. Ainscow, Mel   II. Florek, Anton
  371.9

  ISBN 1-85346-126-1

Typeset by Chapterhouse, Formby
Printed in Great Britain by A. Wheaton & Co., Ltd., Exeter

Contents

SECTION 3 – STAFF DEVELOPMENT

Contributors to the book and current posts held

MEL AINSCOW	Tutor in Special Educational Needs, Cambridge Institute of Education
HEATHER ARTHUR	Deputy County Co-ordinator for TVEI Bedfordshire
PETER BATTY	Teacher Trainer and Consultant Cumbria
HAZEL BINES	Deputy Head of School of Education and Senior Lecturer, Oxford Polytechnic
MARGARET BUCK	Co-ordinator for Special Needs, Tile Hill Wood School, Coventry
SCOTT DUNLOP	Senior Educational Psychologist, Coventry Child Guidance Centre
ANTON FLOREK	Tutor in Special Needs, North East Wales Institute of Higher Education
DAVID GALLOWAY	Lecturer in Educational Research University of Lancaster
JEAN GARNETT	Head of Special Needs Services and Adviser for Special Needs Support Services, Coventry
CAROL GILES	Educational Psychologist, Warwickshire Education Authority
LOIS HOCKLEY	Head of Teaching and Support Service, West Berkshire
ANN HODGSON	Development Manager, Help the Aged, London

BARRY JACKSON Deputy Head, Kingsley School, Kettering

BOB MOON Professor of Education, Open University

JAMES MUNCEY Adviser, Special Educational Needs, Coventry

ANDY REDPATH Headteacher, Moselle School, London Borough of Haringey

CAROLINE ROAF Co-ordinator for Special Needs, Peers School, Littlemore, Oxford

GARY THOMAS Senior Lecturer, School of Education, Oxford Polytechnic

MAVIS WILLEY Head of Heathfield Infants School, London Borough of Richmond-upon-Thames

Preface

This is the first time that articles from the *British Journal of Special Education* have been brought together as a book. Most have been commissioned over the past five years as part of the editors' policy of encouraging a whole school response to pupils with special educational needs. One third of the chapters have not appeared in the journal before; some will do so later.

It is also the first time that the National Council for Special Education has published a book in association with another publisher. We look forward to a successful venture with David Fulton.

The journal will continue to reflect new developments in special educational policy and practice, as it has done over the past 15 years and is continuing to do now in relation to the National Curriculum and the 1988 Education Reform Act. We hope more books based on journal contributions will follow.

The National Council for Special Education and the journal editors are very grateful to Mel Ainscow and Anton Florek, members of the Editorial Board. They have not only edited the book on the NCSE's behalf but have also contributed several of the chapters and introductions to the three sections of the book.

Margaret Peter,
Editor, British Journal of Special Education
July 1989

CHAPTER 1

A Whole School Approach

Mel Ainscow and Anton Florek

Introduction

The *British Journal of Special Education* is the official journal of the National Council for Special Education. As such it provides opportunities for practitioners, teachers and others to talk to one another across its pages. In it they describe their work, share ideas and relate their concerns. Consequently, by reading the journal readers can identify trends and developments in the field of special education.

An increasing trend in recent years has been the move towards meeting children's special educational needs in ordinary primary and secondary schools. Within this trend can also be identified the development of a more specific idea, that of the whole school approach. This is the focus of this book.

The book consists of a selection of articles that have appeared in (or have been recently submitted to) the journal, in which the authors present their experiences and reflections about the idea of a whole school approach to meeting special educational needs. It came about as a result of the Editorial Board's monitoring of the policy of the journal. As part of this work the theme was noted and the idea of a book of readings conceived.

In this introductory chapter we provide a brief account of how the idea of a whole school approach has developed and an explanation of what it means. We then go on to explain how the chapters have been arranged and, in so doing, present themes and issues that should guide readers through the text.

Recent developments

To understand the growing interest in the idea of a whole school approach to meeting special educational needs it is necessary to take account of recent changes in the ways in which the education service responds to children experiencing difficulties in school. Before offering a definition of the idea, therefore, we will provide a summary of these changes.

In a recent book Ainscow and Muncey (1989) analyse developments in the special needs field in terms of the influence of the Warnock Report, a major government-sponsored inquiry into special education that was published in 1978. As the basis of their analysis they draw the distinction between pre- and post-Warnock thinking.

Pre-Warnock thinking, they suggest, was characterised by an emphasis on placing children in categories in order to provide care that tended to be given in segregated settings. This came about as a result of participants within the education service accepting the following assumptions:

(1) A group of children can be identified who are different from the majority.
(2) Only this relatively small group needs special help.
(3) The problems of these children are as a result of their disabilities or personal limitations.
(4) Special help can best be provided when separate groups of children with common problems are taught together.
(5) Once such a group has been provided for, the rest of the school population can be regarded as 'normal'.

Consequently special and remedial education was geared to the identification of particular groups of children thought to have similar problems in order to provide some form of positive discrimination. For some this meant placement in a special school or unit; for many others extra help was provided by withdrawal from lessons in order to provide specialist teaching.

In the post-Warnock era, however, the style has been gradually changing. What we have seen are moves towards approaches that place emphasis on responding to children as individuals through the normal curriculum within contexts characterised by a strong sense of collaboration. This is based upon an acceptance of the Warnock argument that greater numbers of children experience difficulties in the school system than was previously recognised. It is also clear that most of these children are already in ordinary schools. Furthermore, there is a growing trend towards educating youngsters with more severe learning difficulties in the mainstream.

The assumptions behind this new thinking are as follows:

(1) Any child may experience difficulties in school at some stage.
(2) Help and support must be available to all pupils as necessary.
(3) Educational difficulties result from an interaction between what the child brings to the situation and what the school has to offer.
(4) Teachers should take responsibility for the progress of all the children in their classes.
(5) Support must be available to staff as they attempt to meet their responsibilities.

As a result, recent years have seen a reduction of emphasis on trying to find out what is wrong with children. Instead attention is focused on making the curriculum offered to all children more responsive to the needs of individuals. In other words there has been a move away from what might be called a deficit model towards a curriculum-based model for dealing with special educational needs.

Definition

As teachers in many primary and secondary schools have reflected upon this trend and attempted to modify their practice accordingly, the idea of a whole school response has gradually emerged. Inevitably the exact definition of the concept varies from place to place, but always there is the emphasis on responding to children's special educational needs through the school's overall policies. Consequently the approach has implications for all teachers within a school and all aspects of the life of the school.

While various of the writers in this book provide or, at least, imply their own definitions of what they mean by a whole school approach, we will offer our own. It is as follows:

> A whole school approach is where attempts are being made to utilise all the resources of a school to foster the development of all its children.

Thus it can be seen as a part of the move towards comprehensive education – a philosophical thrust to provide equal opportunities for all children and young people.

It is important to note also that our definition is expressed as an aspiration, accepting that practice may fall short of intention. Nevertheless a commitment to this aim of equal opportunity is, in our view, a precursor to improvements in practice. Indeed, while reading through the chapters of this book should act as a source of inspiration, it is also possible to detect the need for a sense of realism, particularly in the light of limited resources.

What this book provides are ideas and suggestions as to how teachers and schools can move towards a whole school approach to meeting children's special educational needs. As such it can be seen as a source of help in facing a series of challenges that are still to be met.

Issues and themes

The articles selected from the journal fall into three groups, each of which addresses broadly the same issue. The three issues are as follows:

● How can whole school policies be developed?
● How can pupils' special educational needs be met in the ordinary classroom?
● How can staff be provided with help and support?

Together these questions provide an agenda that could be used to review the existing policy and practice of a school. In this context, however, they provide a framework within which the chosen articles are presented.

Consequently the three main sections of the book address themes related to these questions. The articles in Section 1 look at the development of school policies; Section 2 is concerned with meeting special educational needs in the classroom; and Section 3 focuses on aspects of staff development. Each of the three sections starts with an editorial overview highlighting key ideas and introducing specific chapters. The concluding chapter provides an opportunity for the editors to speculate about future developments, particularly about the impact of the 1988 Education Act.

References

Ainscow, M. and Muncey, J. (1989) *Meeting Individual Needs in the Primary School*. London: Fulton.

SECTION 1

The Development of School Policies

As schools move towards a whole school approach to meeting special educational needs they are in effect involved in a major curriculum change. Such a change may well require new beliefs and attitudes, new forms of organisation and new skills. It may also involve teachers in taking on new responsibilities, and some of them in adopting new roles within their organisations.

In this first section, therefore, a theme of the chapters is the management of change. In reading these chapters the key question to bear in mind is, how can whole school policies be developed? The various contributors, in describing their own experiences and making recommendations, do not minimise the problems that can occur when complex organisations such as schools attempt to implement significant changes in their practice. Change is a time-consuming process that can easily go wrong and which, despite good intentions, may damage the morale and confidence of those involved. Consequently it has to be managed with care.

None of this is an argument for despondency. As the contributors to this section relate, much has been achieved in many primary and secondary schools. Out of this experience much has been learned that is of benefit to others pursuing the idea of a whole school approach.

In the first chapter in this section Gary Thomas and Barry Jackson give an overview of issues involved in the development of whole school approaches with particular references to staff management. They also provide useful guidelines for minimising problems. Hazel Bines focuses on primary schools, again offering suggestions for development, this time with respect to the development of school policy documents. These suggestions are well illustrated in Mavis Willey's chapter, which is based on her experience as headteacher of an infant school.

Moving the discussion into the secondary field, Peter Batty and his colleagues describe change in special needs provision that occurred over a five-year period at Peers School in Oxfordshire. Their account emphasises the importance of seeing special needs as a curriculum issue. A further example of one secondary school's development is described in the final two chapters of this section by Carol Giles and Scott Dunlop, and by Margaret Buck. Together these chapters provide an in-depth case study of how Tile Hill Wood School in Coventry has moved towards a whole school approach.

CHAPTER 2

The Whole School Approach to Integration

Gary Thomas and Barry Jackson

Moving teachers from special schools and units into the mainstream is like moving the mountain to Mohammed but few would doubt that the payoff for successful upheaval will be enormous for children who have special needs. Using the expertise of 'special' personnel in ordinary classrooms is central to full integration yet scant attention has been paid to how it can be done.

Frequently those practices which are the backbone of special needs provision in *ordinary* schools, like withdrawal, militate against integration. Disguised segregation occurs – on the ordinary school premises . . .

Practices have to be evolved which, *within ordinary schools*, enable those children who are experiencing difficulties to be educated as part of the main body of the school. This means that teachers who have traditionally been responsible for children with learning difficulties will have to seek imaginative ways of spreading their skills to other teachers in the school while simultaneously reaching out to larger numbers of children. The 'whole school' approach, a move of personnel and resources, is one means to this end.

Transposing staff to achieve the whole school approach will usually meet (i) in initiation, institutional constraints to change within the school, and (ii) in practice, the problems which inevitably seem to arise when people share a task. We should like to suggest some guidelines which aim to minimise problems while maximising the chances of moving to a whole school approach and to describe how special needs provision has been integrated at Bicester School.

Problems of implementation

Often educational innovation which has far-reaching effects on the way schools are organised is proposed without a full appreciation of its complexity. Schools are complex organisations whose equilibrium is easily unbalanced. An ill conceived or poorly planned project may not simply fall apart; its débris may be the kind of ill feeling which hinders communication and acts as a barrier to development.

There have been some enlightening accounts of the possible pitfalls which may be encountered in attempts at change. Georgiades and Phillimore (1975), for example, feel that the notion of a 'hero-innovator' in schools is a myth: the truth is that institutions like schools 'eat hero-innovators for breakfast'. They outline strategies which they recommend as encouraging change. Drawing on their advice and that of others (eg Schmuck *et al.*, 1977; Bate, 1984) we should like to suggest points which may lessen the difficulties of this kind of exercise.

(1) The information which will enable teachers to judge the impact of the proposal for themselves should be presented in a concise and digestible form.
(2) It is important to identify *all* those who will be affected by the change – including, of course, the school management – and to canvass their opinions. People are far more likely to work for an innovation if they feel that they have been consulted and that they have contributed to the change.
(3) The scheme should be modified in the light of staff comments.
(4) The scheme should be so designed that it can easily be adapted. Systems which respond to the feedback of users have been shown to have more 'staying power' (qv Robson, 1982).
    At the same time innovators should be sensitive to some facets of the psychology of individuals working in schools.
(5) Therefore, as individuals work better with support, it may be worthwhile establishing a core group of staff who are sympathetic to the whole school notion; the formalising of meetings whereby interested staff can share ideas and ventilate frustrations will help to prevent isolation.
(6) It is better initially to work with what Georgiades and Phillimore

call 'the healthy parts of the system'. Energy will more profitably be expended by starting on a small scale and involving those who are the keenest and the most effective rather than attempting to persuade those who are likely to be cynical about the merits of change.

(7) Last, as the 'hero-innovator' authors suggest, mass public relations exercises are less likely to succeed than modest canvassing of opinion through personal approaches to colleagues. People are more likely to respond positively to some interesting ideas of a colleague than to an assertively 'marketed' whole school package.

Problems of practice

Introducing the new approach to staff is only the beginning. An innovation such as the whole school approach carries with it many problems in practice because it brings together professionals who have customarily worked separately. Territoriality may be a difficulty with some class teachers reacting, if not with hostility, with diffidence to having an additional person in the classroom. Role ambiguity may occur: staff may be uncertain of their own function once additional people are present, and indeed the 'special' staff may not work as effectively as they would wish unless they are quite clear about their role.

Having additional people to help in the ordinary classroom does not on its own solve the problems of children who are experiencing difficulty. Indeed, Ferguson and Adams (1982) have indicated that team teaching among remedial teachers often fails to provide the individual attention that children who are experiencing difficulties require. Similarly DeVault et al. (1977) in a study of personnel involvement in the various Follow Through curricula found that such involvement often resulted in the teacher spending less time with children.

These findings can partly be explained by the phenomenon of diminishing returns. Such diminishing returns may result when more than one person works on a task (with the parameters of the 'task' in this case being the classroom walls) and when each person's input is diminished through, for instance, duplication of effort or getting in the other's way.

While none of these problems is insignificant neither is any of them insurmountable. The problems and their solutions are essentially to do with organisation and management – of resources as well as personnel – in the classroom. The term 'management' in the context of a whole school approach is used to convey a shared exercise in organisational problem-solving. The problem-solving exercise will have to begin with establishing clear role definition. What does seem to be important when more than one person is working in the classroom is that each individual knows what the other is doing; role clarity is the crux of many of the other problems noted. The ideas that follow focus on role delineation.

Importance of role definition

One possible way of delineating the work of different people in the classroom lies in 'room management' procedures devised for use with those who have severe learning difficulties (Porterfield et al., 1977) where high staff–client ratios have allowed more than one person working with a group to be the norm rather than the exception. The system has been successfully used in schools for children with severe learning difficulties (McBrien and Weightman, 1980) and tested with promising results in a top primary classroom (Thomas, 1985).

Although designed for an entirely different environment it has relevance to the whole school approach because it specifies roles. As the system has been described, three roles have been outlined. An 'individual helper' provides intensive help to a series of children, an 'activity manager' focuses on maintaining the engagement of the body of the class, and a 'mover' encourages the flow of work in a session, a function which Kounin (1970) set high in a hierarchy of factors necessary for successful teaching. There is no reason why room management should not be successfully adapted for secondary schools.

Alternative ways of deploying additional staff in the classroom may be found in 'zoning' and in 'person to person' arrangements (LeLaurin and Risley, 1972). The former allocates staff to particular areas of the room, divided by activity, whereas the latter makes particular personnel responsible for specific children.

These models each have their strengths and weaknesses. (For a full discussion of the rationale behind their use and a description of their operation, see Thomas, 1986.) Suffice it to say here that room management appears to enable individual help to be given while the focus of the group is successfully maintained, two basic classroom needs which it is notoriously difficult to reconcile. Zoning may be more useful where there is much transfer from one activity to another in the room, while person to person arrangements, in allowing for consistent pairing of an adult to a group of children, make for the sort of stability of relationship which might be considered important for children with emotional difficulties being integrated into ordinary classrooms.

Theory into practice

We should now like to describe the successful inception of a plan for delivering the skills of a remedial department to the whole school which began in the summer term of 1985. Bicester School is a medium sized (five to six form entry) comprehensive which relied on a conventional system of withdrawal from the foundation studies department and academic departments for children who had special educational needs. The foundation studies department provides an integrated curriculum within a mixed ability framework for all first and second year pupils. From the third year onwards this structure gives way to organisation via academic departments.

Although 'special needs' coexisted harmoniously with the various departments, sensitivity to the whole school ideals noted earlier in this article prompted an acceptance that structural change was necessary if those ideals were to be realised. Such structural change was realised in the formation of a new department – the Educational Resource and Support (ERS) Department – which sought to support teachers in ordinary classes. In sketching the procedures adopted to bring about the changes, we shall outline the various phases in the introduction, induction and implementation of changes.

Phase 1: Fact finding

It was felt important that staff at the school be given a detailed and objective appraisal of ideas and opinions from both inside and outside the school on the reshaping of special needs provision. The head of the remedial department was able to marshal information on innovations elsewhere while attending Oxford Polytechnic for one of the DES's 4/84 (DES, 1984) courses. Internal evaluation of the existing organisation and structure of special needs within the school examined who was responsible for what; who meets whom; why they meet, and so forth. This initial analysis threw up many ambiguities and anomalies; for example, three members of staff could be writing to one set of parents about a particular problem. Making explicit the nature of problems which had previously been tacitly known made everyone more receptive to ideas about changes in the system.

Phase 2: Regular feedback to senior management

An innovation such as this clearly cannot take place without the support of the senior management of the school. Like any other staff, they are likely to respond more favourably to the notion of change where the reasons for it are fully explained and when they help to plan it. At Bicester School a weekly meeting was held with the headteacher and he was kept fully involved in planning.

Phase 3: Seeking opinions of staff

As already stated, teachers are much more likely to accept change if they see that the idea has been carefully thought out and if they are given the chance to discuss it fully in advance. It is no use springing the proposals on the headteacher on a Friday afternoon and expecting that the innovation can be made in isolation from the staff who will be affected by it. Consequently, the head of special needs wrote a discussion paper outlining recent thinking in special education and giving reasons for the move to a whole school approach by some schools. The discussion document served three primary functions.

(1) It kept all those who would be affected informed of proposed changes.
(2) It cleared up misunderstandings about the proposals. Foundation studies staff were concerned, for example, that a reduction of withdrawal would reduce time available for exploring more complex aspects of the curriculum which might arise, for instance, out of 'Man, a Course of Study'. Some academic departments were concerned about handing over to special needs staff responsibility for creating resources within their subject area. It was possible to explain to them that ERS staff would not be interfering with the curriculum but rather would be adapting its presentation in order to give larger numbers of children access to it.
(3) It enabled staff to suggest changes in the model.

This exercise also helped in deflecting criticism of the scheme by staff as being merely the activity of an 'empire builder'. This applied to senior management as much as to any other staff; headteachers are under constant pressure, often arising from inter-departmental conflict within their schools. It is within this context that management have to assess a number of worthy schemes put to them. One major advantage of suggesting an innovation whose induction has been worked through in this way is that senior management will immediately be less unsure about reception of the idea by the staff.

Phase 4: Presentation

After fact finding and consultation, a finalised document could be presented to the staff which incorporated a large number of variations and amendments. Given the involvement of the staff throughout it was possible confidently to support and defend the final scheme. That scheme meant abandoning the existing organisation for special needs in favour of the new ERS Department which subsumed and merged the bipartite strands ('progress' and 'behaviour') of the old system. Integral to that reformulation was the setting up of a *key coordinators' committee* which has promoted the linking of pastoral and academic functions in the school. This committee was written into the school's management structure.

A final meeting for representatives from the school management, the curriculum development committee, and the foundation studies department (which would be much affected by the change) took place. After discussion staff generally agreed that the ideas within the final document stood a good chance of working.

Phase 5: Giving the innovation status

Especially in a traditionally low status area like special needs, it is not enough to introduce an innovation that affects all members of staff and to expect the special needs staff effectively to implement the changes on their own. This problem has been avoided by establishing that a *deputy head* would chair the new special needs coordinators' committee; this has given the committee both status and a mandate to invoke new procedures.

This internal committee was arranged to dovetail with a fortnightly external agencies committee – also chaired by the deputy head and attended by the head of ERS. Thus the deputy head would have a close working knowledge of trials and tribulations of the head of ERS; they would work together to carry out suggested courses of action. The committee is concerned, among other tasks, with floating new ideas which may assist the smooth working of a whole school ideal. A recent example has been the agreement with year tutors that for certain children a 'named person' from ERS will liaise with agencies and parents on matters where there is the greatest chance of ambiguity about who is responsible for what.

Phase 6: Maintenance

In order to maintain the vitality and coherence of the system, we hope to extend outside the small special needs team the notion of cooperation and teamwork for the benefit of special needs children. The special needs staff will therefore visit the year and departmental teams in rotation once a fortnight. They will discuss (i) certain specific children in the school who have special educational needs and (ii) the running of the new system.

Phase 7: Practice

Consistent with the advice outlined earlier, none of the teamwork models (room management, zoning, person to person) has been imposed on methods of working in the classroom. Rather, the hope is that one of the models might be the starting point for adaptations uniquely suited to the needs of the children and staff of any particular class. With such an aim in mind the head of the ERS has made a schematic representation of the models for display on the staff notice board and invited staff to discuss with him methods of working based upon them.

Conclusion

So far the accounts which exist of personnel integration (eg Hodgson *et al.*, 1984) have been descriptive rather than analytic. This perhaps reflects the fact that changes from the work style familiar to most of us confront us with unfamiliar problems.

However, warnings concerning organisational change need not be taken too weightily. Appreciating the difficulties should not deter us from finding and evaluating more effective ways of helping children with special needs, through the *delivering* of the knowledge and skill of remedial teachers to them.

We hope that the whole school approach will increasingly find favour in schools. While the terrain in this diversion may be unfamiliar for most of us working in special education, the way is by no means uncharted and the destination holds promise for those children who are experiencing difficulty.

[This article was first published in *British Journal of Special Education* Volume 13, No. 1: March 1986.]

References

Bate, P. (1984) 'The impact of organizational culture on approaches to organizational problem solving'. *Organization Studies*, 5, 1, 43–66.

DeVault, M. L., Harnischfeger, A. and Wiley, D. E. (1977) *Curricula, Personnel Resources and Grouping Strategies*. St. Ann, Mo.: ML-GROUP for Policy Studies in Education. (ED 155151).

DES (1984) *The In-service Teacher Training Grants Scheme*. (Circular No 4/84). London: HMSO.

Ferguson, N. and Adams, M. (1982) 'Assessing the advantages of team teaching in remedial education: the remedial teacher's role.' *Remedial Education*, 17, 1: 24–30.

Georgiades, N. J. and Phillimore, L. (1975) 'The myth of the hero-innovator and alternative strategies for organizational change'. In C. C. Kiernan and F. P. Woodford (eds.) *Behaviour Modification with the Severely Retarded*. Amsterdam: Associated Scientific.

Hodgson, A., Clunies-Ross, L. and Hegarty, S. (1984) *Learning Together: Teaching Pupils with Special Educational Needs in the Ordinary School*. Windsor: NFER-Nelson.

Kounin, J. S. (1970) *Discipline and Group Management in Classrooms*. NY: Holt, Rinehart and Winston.

LeLaurin, K. and Risley, T. R. (1972) 'The organisation of day care environments: "zone" v "man to man" staff assignments'. *Journal of Applied Behaviour Analysis*, 5, 3: 225–232.

McBrien, J. and Weightman, J. (1980) 'The effect of room managements procedures on the engagement of profoundly retarded children'. *British Journal of Mental Subnormality*, 26, 1.

Porterfield, J., Blunden, R. and Blewitt, E. (1977) *Improving Environments for Profoundly Handicapped Adults: establishing staff routines for high client engagement*. Cardiff: Mental Handicap in Wales Applied Research Unit, Univ. College, Cardiff.

Robson, M. (1982) *Quality Circles: A Practical Guide*. Aldershot: Gower.

Schmuck, R. A., Runkel, P. J., Arends, J. H. and Arends, R. I. (1977) *The Second Handbook of Organization Development in Schools*. Palo Alto: Mayfield.

Thomas, G. (1985) 'Room management in mainstream education'. *Educational Research*, 27, 3: 186–194.

Thomas, G. (1986) 'Integrating personnel in order to integrate children'. *Support for Learning*, 1, 1: 19–26.

CHAPTER 3

Developing a Whole School Policy for Special Needs in Primary Schools

Hazel Bines

The 'whole school' approach to special educational provision in both secondary and primary schools is now widely accepted as a good model of practice. Drawing on the framework established by the 1981 Education Act and the Warnock Report, this model deploys a broad and interactive concept of special needs and is concerned with the involvement of all teachers within a school in identifying and providing for special needs. It also includes a different role for special needs teachers in that the traditional focus on the assessment and remediation of learning and other difficulties has been extended to include a supportive and advisory brief across the whole curriculum (Bines, 1986; NARE, 1985). Support services are similarly moving from providing extra remedial help for children towards also offering support and advisory work (Gipps *et al*. 1987; Laskier, 1985).

The implementation of this model in secondary schools has been well documented, with a number of accounts of how former remedial departments have developed new policies (e.g. Daniels, 1984; Lewis, 1984; Thomas and Jackson, 1986). Suggestions as to how primary schools might develop a similar approach have not been so widely available although recent publications have begun to usefully fill this gap (e.g. Wolfendale, 1987). Primary schools may thus have to develop their own ideas and practices, particularly since experience of the secondary model cannot be applied wholesale to the primary sector because of differences in curriculum and organisation. In addition, despite widespread acceptance of this model, it is still not entirely clear what a 'whole school approach' or 'whole school policy' should comprise and how it should be developed. For example, there is the question of whether such a policy should primarily be an ethos or way of working or also involve formal documentation. There is also the problem of what a policy should particularly include. Should it, for example, be largely concerned with questions of principle or of procedure? Should it focus on roles and responsibilities of staff or on curriculum and teaching methods? And should it include all aspects of practice such as relationships with parents, integration programmes and the role of other professionals? In addition, effective ways of fostering and implementing such a policy have to be found. Currently, of course, there is also the question of how the development of whole school policies on special needs will mesh with implementation of the National Curriculum and assessment.

Development of a whole school policy

Nevertheless there are a number of potential guidelines for developing such a policy. Firstly, any form of whole school policy would seem to involve values and ethos, together with the change and support of relevant attitudes and behaviours (Roaf, 1988) and there is no reason to think that a policy on special needs would be different in this respect. Indeed, a special needs policy would seem to fall into the category of policies particularly concerned with equality and rights, and thus with values, beliefs and ethos (Roaf, *ibid*.). Secondly, because of wide consensus on its importance, coupled with the thrust of the 1981 Education Act, integration is likely to be a crucial element of such a policy, including both children from special schools and the 'eighteen per cent' of those with special needs who have always been in ordinary primary schools. This should involve not just integration of children but integration of the curriculum (Lewis, 1988), particularly since curriculum is now largely seen as the central pivot of special needs work (Clough and Thompson, 1987).

Thirdly, coordination and management are likely to have to be considered, particularly the roles and responsibilities of classteachers, the headteacher and the special needs coordinator. This aspect of policy needs to reflect the supportive and advisory brief for special needs teachers/coordinators outlined earlier. In relation to the special needs coordinator in particular, consideration could also be given to the role of any curriculum consultant within a primary school. In recent years, as Campbell (1985) amongst others has pointed out, the role of primary postholders has changed from being concerned mostly with resources towards development of the curriculum through postholder-led collaboration. This has meant the development of a more collegial model of management. The curriculum consultant is now seen as a major figure in primary schools (Alexander, 1984; Campbell, *op.cit.*) – a management structure which is likely to be further developed and reinforced in the implementation of the National Curriculum. The collaborative and curricular orientation of both general primary management and special needs approaches should thus be particularly useful in developing this aspect of policy on special needs. Finally, it is probable that a policy would incorporate commitment to the involvement of parents, reflecting both legislation and professional consensus on the importance of this aspect of a school's work.

Despite such general guidelines, however, the development of policy may generate certain problems. It cannot be assumed, for example, that there will be consensus on values or ethos, or even on major issues such as integration. The exercise of the responsibilities of special needs coordinators also involves a number of potential difficulties. Probably the most important is having enough time to implement the role given major commitments to class teaching. It may also be difficult to change the practice of colleagues. Both these and other difficulties have been experienced by curriculum coordinators in general (Campbell, *ibid.*) but may be more acute in relation to special needs. The development of support for children with special needs in mainstream classrooms, for example, raises many issues about team teaching and giving advice (Hart, 1986; Thomas, 1985). Experience of implementing support work in the secondary sector also suggests that there may be differences in teaching approach and relationships with children to be resolved, as well as the anxieties and concerns which may be experienced by those not used to consultation or teamwork (Bines, *op.cit.*). In some schools there may not even be a recognised special needs coordinator, or the responsibilities may be attached to another role, such as responsibility for language within the curriculum, or the deputy headship. There may in some instances be part-time remedial teaching help or other support services but it is probably generally the case that those who do have responsibility for special needs will have to carry out their work whilst also being a class teacher, and/or in conjunction with other roles. The possibilities for direct, classroom based curriculum and policy development by the special needs coordinator are thus likely to be somewhat constrained.

The development of a whole school policy document may therefore provide one means of overcoming some of the difficulties outlined above. It would enable schools to specifically focus on the development of curriculum and other aspects of practice and ensure discussion of the different issues involved. Some more detailed suggestions will thus now be made about the possible components of a policy on special needs.

Components of a policy document

There are a number of potential approaches to producing such a document. Issues of ethos, integration, curriculum, coordination and management, and parental involvement have already been briefly discussed. Wolfendale has suggested that a policy should include home-school links and parental participation; management of learning; behaviour management; organisation of school, classroom and curriculum; staff development and support; liaison with support services (1987, p. 125). My own work on this issue in initial and in-service training has used ten identified areas of policy. These are: general aims and ethos (including integration); staff roles and responsibilities; assessment and record keeping; curriculum; resources; pastoral care and behaviour management; working with parents; working with support agencies; staff development; policy review. The most important issue, of course, is not trying to find some model policy headings which will fit all situations but rather covering each aspect of special needs provision in an effective way in a particular school. However, given that the development of a few 'model policies' might provide some very useful guidelines, some more specific suggestions on content will now be made.

- The **general aims and ethos** of a policy ought perhaps to be clearly stated, so that staff and parents are aware of guiding principles. Each school will wish to establish its own aims and ethos, although it is likely that issues of integration, equal opportunities, provision for individual needs, the full development of children's potential and an appropriate entitlement for children with special needs will be important issues which need to be raised.
- Once such aims have been established, **roles and responsibilities** can then be discussed. This part of the policy ought to include the role of all teachers, of the special needs coordinator and of the

head and deputy. It could include quite detailed descriptions of responsibilities, to ensure good communication and management. Discussion of this area of the policy also provides opportunities to stress the responsibility of all teachers in relation to ensuring effective provision as well as ways in which the school will fulfil its legal obligations under the 1981 and 1988 Education Acts in relation to special needs.

- The most substantial part of the policy will probably be concerned with educational provision, including **assessment and recordkeeping, curriculum** and **resources**. Discussion and decision making are likely to focus on: diagnostic and other tests used, including who should administer them and who should record and monitor children's general progress; development of a 'curriculum for all' together with providing for individual needs (learning, behaviour and impairment) within group and class teaching; teaching methods and approaches; support for children in class and through additional help; cooperative teaching; resources for learning and teaching. Reference may be made to other curricular issues such as multicultural education and language teaching provision. Issues of how special needs provision relates to the curriculum provided as a whole should be a key focus, and in future considerable attention will have to be paid to the National Curriculum and stages of assessment. Staff responsibilities and parental involvement are also likely to have to be considered within this part of the policy, thus linking with other areas within the policy as a whole.

- Questions of **pastoral care and behaviour management** are likely to be recurrent themes in the above aspects of a policy, but may also merit specific consideration as a discrete area of a document.

- Approaches to **working with parents and with support services** such as educational psychologists and speech therapists could then be given more detailed examination, including such issues as who initiates and monitors cooperation and liaison and who will encourage the further involvement of parents whose children may have special needs. Where appropriate, staff may also wish to consider any specific programmes of integration, for example integrating children in collaboration with a local special school.

- Finally, specific aspects of **staff development** could be identified and a programme of in-service training outlined, together with a process of **policy review** through which a school can both review its own policy and respond to LEA and national policy initiatives and changes.

Developing and using a policy in schools

Schools will have a number of ways of developing their particular policies, for example through staff meetings, working documents and individual consultation. Such policy development may take place alongside other initiatives or may be chosen as the key focus of discussion and activity for a period. It is likely that the special needs coordinator will play a key role, working in conjunction with other curriculum consultants and the headteacher. Experience of policy development in general suggests that the document is likely to be written over a period of time and that staff consultation and involvement are more important than a quickly completed or highly polished statement. It is thus important to recognise that a policy can never be a totally finished document or be imposed on staff and school. Rather, as Alexander (1984) has suggested, it is better viewed as a 'working paper'

> which is the product of substantial collective discussion and is subjected to regular review and modification in the light of both the experience of implementing it and of changing circumstances (p. 195).

– an approach which, as Alexander goes on to note, is also argued by HMI.

Such a cooperative and flexible approach will of course be more time-consuming. However, commitment to the policy is more likely if there is involvement and the confidence that the policy does indeed reflect the needs of the school.

The degree to which such a policy will be highly prescriptive or rather act as a more general guideline is likely to depend on the particular needs and approach of a particular school. However it is probable that the policy will be most effective if it is fairly detailed. A school should also consider how it is going to make that policy available to parents and to support services linked to the school and how they too can be involved in discussion.

Once a 'working document' has been written, it could be put to a number of uses in addition to its function as a general guide to practice. It could, for example, be used as a basis for informing parents about approaches to and provision for special needs within the school. It could also be used as a tool for school self-evaluation, in terms of the degree to which the aims and content of the document are realised in practice. It may also provide a useful reference point for the LEA and other bodies and services concerned with the school. Its most important value, however, rests in the process involved in generating the policy, and the consequences for teaching and learning as the policy is implemented.

Conclusion

Development of a whole school policy document, therefore, could be regarded as a useful and important method of clarifying and developing ethos, provision and practice in relation to special needs. Given the wide range of demands now being made on teachers in primary schools, a working policy could help to focus attention on special needs and ensure integration of this part of a school's overall policy with the many other aspects of a whole school's work. Coupled with local and national exchange of practice and experience between primary schools, it could help considerably to enhance and encourage the whole school approach to special needs in primary education.

[This article was first published in *British Journal of Special Education* Volume 16, No. 2: March 1986.]

References

Alexander, R. J. (1984) *Primary Teaching*. London: Holt, Rinehart and Winston.

Bines, H. (1986) *Redefining Remedial Education*. Beckenham: Croom Helm.

Campbell, R. J. (1985) *Developing the Primary School Curriculum*. London: Holt, Rinehart and Winston.

Clough, P. and Thompson, D. (1987) 'Curricular approaches to learning difficulties: Problems for the paradigm', in Franklin, B. (Ed) *Learning Disabilities: Dissenting Essays*. Lewes: Falmer Press.

Daniels, E. (1984) 'A suggested model of remedial provision in a comprehensive school'. *Remedial Education*, **19**, 2: 78–83.

Gipps, C., Gross, H. and Goldstein, H. (1987) *Warnock's Eighteen Per Cent*. Lewes: Falmer Press.

Hart, S. (1986) 'Evaluating support teaching'. *Gnosis*, **9**: 26–31.

Laskier, M. (1985) 'The changing role of the remedial teacher', in Smith, C. J. (Ed) *New Directions in Remedial Education*. Lewes: Falmer Press.

Lewis, A. (1988) 'Children with special needs in primary schools' in Clarkson, M. (Ed) *Emerging Issues in Primary Education*. Lewes: Falmer Press.

Lewis, G. (1984) 'A supportive role at secondary level'. *Remedial Education*, **19**, 1: 7–12.

NARE (National Association for Remedial Education) (1985) *Guidelines No 6 Teaching Roles for Special Educational Needs*. Stafford: NARE.

Roaf, C. (1988) 'The concept of a whole school approach to special needs' in Robinson, O. (Ed) *Tackling Learning Difficulties*. London: Hodder and Stoughton.

Thomas, G. (1986) 'Integrating personnel in order to integrate children'. *Support for Learning* **1**, 1: 19–26.

Thomas, G. and Jackson, B. (1986) 'The whole school approach to integration'. *British Journal of Special Education*, **13**, 1: 27–9.

Wolfendale, S. (1987) *Primary Schools and Special Needs*. London: Cassell.

CHAPTER 4

Moving from Policy to Practice

Mavis Willey

A whole school approach can be seen as the philosophy and practice of a group of individuals who agree on how to meet collectively the whole range of needs of the children in their school. Agreeing in principle to the philosophy of this approach is unlikely to be a problem. It is agreement about practice, about the content and how to put it into action, where the difficulties are likely to begin. The account which follows is an attempt to show ways in which a whole school approach might be introduced in primary schools, drawing on my experience over 20 years in introducing this kind of policy into three infant schools in the London area. It is also intended as a sharing of experience on some of the problems which can arise (and which can usually be overcome), particularly those incidents which, in retrospect, cause heads and others to shudder with discomfiture.

Who takes the initiative?

The initiative for proposing a whole school policy for meeting children's needs can come from several sources. It may arise from class teachers who see a need for more continuity and consistency, from class to class, in responding to problems like children's behaviour, their language or literacy needs and, most recently, the implementation of the National Curriculum. Alternatively it may come from the headteacher, perhaps one who has recently arrived at the school, or from a group of senior staff although these sources, in my experience, are less effective. Teachers may feel changes are being imposed on them. Either way, the awareness that such an approach needs to be introduced will have come gradually. Whole school approaches do not spring up overnight.

Reaching an agreement on the principle

Once the suggestion has been floated informally it can be put to a meeting of the whole staff, care assistants and others included. What we may now label as a whole school approach flows naturally from good practice in the primary school and staff are likely to welcome the idea. If they are encouraged to play an active part in formulating and implementing plans they are more likely to feel a sense of ownership of the plans which evolve, to carry out changes with enthusiasm and not to regard the policy as a set of documents to be stacked away in a cupboard until an inspector or the headteacher insists on bringing them out for a temporary airing. Agreement in principle to adopting the whole school approach may therefore be reached quite quickly over one or two staff meetings but I have also known it to take longer, particularly if fears about loss of professional autonomy are voiced. Whatever they may be, doubts and fears must be brought out if they arise at this stage and if they cannot be resolved immediately another meeting can be held a few days later, giving time for all the staff to look again at their own practice and the proposals.

Reaching agreement on practice: a first project

Once agreement to the principle has been reached the next – and more challenging – stage is to reach mutual consent as to the content and practice of the whole school approach. The question for the next staff meeting is 'Where shall we begin?' It is clearly impossible to tackle all aspects of school life simultaneously so a starting point – a first project – has to be found.

While it is tempting to begin by tackling a major issue identified by all staff the temptation must be resisted, as I have found over the past 20 years. There is usually a series of sound reasons why such issues have not been resolved. It is a shared and painful experience that the easiest way to demotivate staff is to tackle an issue in urgent need of change. A controversial issue is likely to provoke conflict and discord which could become the graveyard of the whole school approach. It is far better to find a starting point where there is already some agreement about policy and where there is a nucleus of good practice on which to build. In this way the foundations for agreement can be firmly established without the risks of confusion and complexity.

At the next meeting to discuss the whole school approach staff can be asked for suggestions about where to begin, bearing in mind the need to look for an area where some agreement exists. All proposals need to be minuted for current or future consideration and all proposals need to be treated with respect and listened to, *however* idiosyncratic they may seem. Unless an atmosphere of mutual trust and respect is being built up at this time doubts and fears are left unexpressed and may grow into resentments which undermine future plans.

The choice of a starting point depends on the circumstances of the individual school. At Rotherfield, my previous infant school, which was a combined nursery and infant school for over 200 pupils, we decided to begin with children's behaviour, which had been causing general concern and which everyone agreed was ripe for improvement. There was a developing policy which promised success but needed clarification and consistency. In another school the starting point might be a common marking policy – a very useful way of generating discussion on meeting all children's needs. Whatever is suggested, however, some teachers are likely to disagree initially and it may take another meeting or two before everyone is in accord.

It is also important, around this time or certainly during the first project, to be aware of the group dynamics in such a situation – what some would call 'forming, storming and norming'. A group with a common, whole school aim has begun to form but my experience so far suggests that the next stage – 'storming' – is impossible to avoid. So listening to the protests and criticisms and discussing each in turn is essential if the group is to settle down to a 'norm' of working together in harmony towards a shared aim.

Drawing up guidelines: the next stage

Once the starting point has been agreed a working party can be formed to look at the way this proposal for a first project can be translated into guidelines for future policy. In my experience the working party should not exceed eight members; in a much smaller school all members of the teaching staff might be able to take part. The size is important. Eight to 10 members is probably the maximum if the guidelines are to be moved forward quickly.

It may take the working party several meetings before it can agree on a draft document to present to the whole staff. This is one of the most demanding stages, when staff are getting down to the 'nitty-gritty' of what needs to be done, when they are suggesting approaches and procedures which some teachers will see as threatening to their autonomy and long established practices. It is likely to take a good deal of patient listening and talking through potential sticking points before the guidelines are ready in draft form.

Our own guidelines, at Rotherfield Infant School, reiterated our commitment to a whole school policy, looked at the behaviour patterns of children who were causing problems and provided a checklist of factors both at home and at school which seemed likely to have a bearing on how pupils behaved. They offered advice on helping and responding to the children, including suggested dialogues, emphasised the management of behaviour through positive reinforcement, and encouraged staff to try out the ideas and to tape record their performance.

Resolving deadlocks about where to begin

If it is clear at a staff meeting that agreement cannot be reached, I have found it better to terminate a discussion rather than to allow a dominant member of the staff to end up by dictating an unpopular policy when sheer exhaustion causes unwilling agreement. Policies decided in such circumstances are rarely sustained. So it is best to end the meeting by stating and recording the areas of agreement and then to identify clearly the areas where there is dissent and where staff could usefully collect more information on the suggested lines of action, reflect and experiment over several days to see if they can come closer to agreeing a common aim.

Such strategies can be very simple. For example, teachers can complete a daily diary and a checklist and write a short statement on the proposals which have been made. At the next staff meeting their observations and reflections can be shared and from these it is usually possible at last to come to some agreement on the first project.

This strategy certainly succeeded in another school where I have worked. The school decided to work on language policy as its first project, and lengthy arguments arose about whether to use a skills-based approach or one based on children's developmental stages, particularly in writing. After the meeting teachers went off to observe what actually improved the content of the children's writing and its transcription. At the next meeting there was much more agreement and the seeds of the project were sown, from which aims and practices could grow, linked into existing language policies.

Even these strategies for agreement may occasionally fail. It may sometimes be wiser to follow the preferences of certain members of staff, idiosyncratic though these may seem, rather than relentlessly pursuing a reasoned argument to what could turn out to be a bitter end. It is impossible to *impose* a whole school policy on others. Unless it is done gradually and by general consent the whole school policy will divide and fail. So willingness to compromise in order to move ahead may be better than risking deadlock. An independent observer can also be a help, as one of my previous schools found when trying to tackle work forecasts for a whole school approach. We had become so caught up in differences of opinion that we had neglected many areas of common agreement – until these were pointed out by the observer and were acted on.

Occasionally when one person, despite all persuasion, rejects the proposals it is important to listen to the objections, to record them, and to promise to return to them at the next annual review. The objections usually ebb away well before the 12 months is up or the majority viewpoint is accepted after further consideration. It is usually a matter of attaining a balance rather than insisting on radical reform.

Agreeing the guidelines and taking action

The next – and equally challenging – step is to present the draft guidelines to the entire staff, including nursery nurses and others. Through long experience I have found it essential to emphasise that the guidelines are only in draft form and that they can be changed. This is another stage at which staff may begin to realise how the proposed policy could affect their own principles and practice. Again doubts can emerge and fears about loss of professional autonomy re-surface. The forcibly expressed preferences of, say, a new deputy head or a very dominant group of staff can bring ill feeling and lead to a polarisation of attitudes which spells the death of the whole school policy before it has yet begun.

It is vital, therefore, to have a skilled chairperson to run the meetings at which the draft guidelines are presented to the staff – possibly someone seen as 'neutral' from another school or another sector of the education service.

It is equally important to keep the meetings to a pre-arranged length of, say, one to $1\frac{1}{2}$ hours. Any issues which are not resolved can be kept for next time. It is useful to organise two staff meetings in quick succession. After an initial meeting, and a night for reflection, it is surprising how much better discussion often goes the following day. Strengths and weaknesses of the proposed guidelines have become more apparent and the second staff meeting allows these to be identified and moves the discussion quickly forward. Sometimes a longer gap may be needed so that teachers can reflect on points of dis agreement and have time to try out some of the classroom practices being suggested.

Agreement on adopting the guidelines may not, however, come until one to two months (and many revisions) later. To arrive triumphantly at this point may depend on convincing the less enthusiastic 'whole schoolers' that the guidelines are not 'set in stone', that they are a working document that will be reviewed in a year's time. In this way staff anxieties are usually allayed and the possibility of subsequent changes ensured. After guidelines have been amended at a series of meetings a review meeting can then be called to approve a final version of the guidelines – complete with deletions and additions by all or many of the staff.

Putting guidelines into action

The next stage is to circulate the guidelines in their final form to everyone in the school, giving a launching date – perhaps the beginning of the following week – for implementation and a date for review in a year's time. It is important that the existing school policy continues right up to the date for introducing the new approach. Chaos and confusion can ensue if staff begin to implement it at different times.

Reaching this point may take up to a term. However, once implementation begins peace and purposefulness usually reign as staff work to the guidelines. During this period they are 'fine-tuning' the policy and noting suggestions for improvements which they can make at the first annual review.

Beginning subsequent projects

Once the first project is strongly rooted it should be possible, a term or two later, to begin looking at another area where a whole school policy can be introduced. Launching a second (and subsequent) project can be a good deal easier now that the ground has been prepared and the prickles cleared. This is the point at which a parent-governor or other parent representative can be invited to join the working party. I have found parent support to be essential to a successful whole school policy and parents may need to be reassured that the new policies are not some kind of palace revolution, and that the changes have developed out of previous practice rather than representing a break with the past.

Once a second project has been agreed and is underway, a third and then a fourth can be added over a period of, say, three or four years until most of the major school activities become part of the whole school approach. It is remarkable how the experience of success on the first project helps bring enthusiasm and agreement for the ones which follow.

Later projects may, for instance, relate to literacy, the organisation of teaching, or practical arrangements for design technology or other activities. In my present school, a nursery/infant school with over 300 pupils and a language unit with 10 children, we are now looking at the National Curriculum from the whole school viewpoint, and a series of working parties is preparing reports. These focus on the school's current guidelines for maths, language and science, with the format and content being changed to incorporate the National Curriculum. The school's policy, designed to meet its particular needs, is central. The policies laid down in the draft documents will be tried out by the whole school during the summer term with each teacher concentrating on the age group he or she is teaching. At the end of the summer term changes may be made to the policy in the light of our experience and developments in the National Curriculum. As usual, a review date will be set for a year ahead, during the summer term of 1990.

The future

The arrival of the National Curriculum, local management of schools, and other changes dictated by the Education Reform Act, will inevitably influence the whole school approach in future.

Staff at Heathfield generally see the National Curriculum as an interesting challenge to fit into the whole school approach. The widely based programmes of study and attainment targets for maths, science and English (the foundation subjects thus covered so far) promise to allow all children's needs and interests to be met within the context of a whole school policy and one of the current issues for discussion is how to improve ways of organising teaching so that children are enabled to work at different levels on the National Curriculum while being in the same class. Now that a national curricular framework has been laid down teachers welcome the opportunity to spend more time on classroom organisation and other aspects of teaching and to find the most effective ways to deliver the curriculum at various levels to children within their class. A sense of excitement, clarity and continuity is beginning to emerge from beneath the panic of the short time left before implementation in September.

The flexible use of resources which local management of schools should allow in future should make it easier to arrange in-service training to support a whole school approach. It might, for instance, be possible for a school to engage a maths specialist for a term to help in the implementation of a maths policy for all children and to direct teaching and other resources towards various groups of children and various curriculum areas at varying times, as the need arises.

Conclusions

Moving towards a whole school approach can be seen as an organic process where the first initiatives can set up a chain of positive events, enabling a school to move forwards towards a commonly agreed policy which meets needs of all children.

Progress towards this ideal needs, however, to be carefully planned, done gradually, and with due regard for individual opinions and differences. Flexibility in drawing up guidelines for a whole school policy and allowance for regular reviews are essential as I have tried to indicate above. The written guidelines at Heathfield are always seen as being in draft form and space is allowed on the written sheets for staff to comment and to record ideas for improvements. Opportunity for change is an essential feature of a successful whole school policy.

After 20 years' experience of introducing a whole school approach into schools I am convinced of its advantages. The feelings of 'ownership' which joint decision making and planning of school policy induce in teachers enable the approach to be the most effective way for knowledge to be translated into action and to ensure continuity of policy and practices.

Despite teachers' fears at the beginning, particularly about loss of their professional autonomy, we have found the reverse to be true. Once the approach has been implemented and its aims made clear it has united staff rather than dividing them. It has brought them together to share their experience of working towards the same ideal. The flexibility of the approach enables the complex matrix of different and changing learning styles among children, rates of learning, individual interests and strengths to be accommodated. At its best I have found that the whole school approach helps to develop a good self-image in children and to encourage all pupils to appreciate one another's contributions.

CHAPTER 5

Changing the Curriculum at Peers

Peter Batty, Bob Moon, Caroline Roaf

Can curriculum reform encourage the introduction of a whole school policy on meeting special needs? Our experience at Peers School where, over five years, both the curriculum and special needs provision have undergone fundamental change, suggests it can.

Peers is a 10-form entry (former grammar) school for 900 pupils aged 13 to 18, serving the British Leyland area of Oxford City, where the curriculum in the early 1980s differed little from that of many other schools in the country. It consisted of a compulsory core (English, mathematics, physical education and religious education), with six options. The top line of this, significantly, represented almost subject for subject the grammar school curriculum of Littlemore Grammar School in 1958, with the descending columns representing the descending academic hierarchy. At the bottom were to be found the institutionalised ideas which arose from the Newsom Report (1963) and raising of the school leaving age initiatives of the Sixties and Seventies. At the very bottom of the columns, spanning four of them, featured the vocational skills course, run by the special needs department for dissenters and dropouts in the system. It is of interest partly as a final comment on the academic hierarchy and partly because it was here that a modular approach was first piloted at Peers. If the starting point for change in the curriculum at Peers had been the school's self evaluation, then just completed, its justification lay in a critique of the comprehensive system as it has developed over the past 20 years.

Background to introduction of new initiatives

We have inherited a comprehensive curriculum that is rooted in the historical notion that comprehensive education would be grammar school education for all. From the start, this has been a major determinant of curricular practice in comprehensives, both in terms of the structure that has evolved (a grammar school structure with the rest built on underneath), and in the criteria for judging success within it (academic criteria).

It is important to recognise that there is nothing wrong with academic disciplines *per se*: rather it is the structural influence which they have exerted on the curriculum which is so wicked, for this has meant we have inherited a curriculum determined by tradition rather than learning theory. Its effect has been to lock students into classrooms for two years on courses selected at 13-plus largely for the sake of administrative convenience – choices which rarely turn out to be completely right for the individuals; courses to which they are rarely ideally suited – but essentially choices and courses from which there is no retreat.

Consider, too, the outcomes of this curriculum for the students. In a set-up which has been determined by academic aspirations for all it is not surprising to find a public examination system playing the dominant role and the important point to note about this is the degree to which failure is built into the courses leading up to public examinations, not to mention the examinations themselves.

Two illustrations will help: in 1985, according to DES figures, the average number of passes in the Certificate of Secondary Education (CSE) Grade 5 and above was 5.6. In itself this is quite a respectable figure, no doubt, but consider it against the number of courses *embarked on* two years earlier, which is likely to have been nine or 10, and you get a failure rate of around 40 per cent. Remember also that until recently we have not even thought about, let alone offered, a nationally validated alternative method of recognising achievement. The second illustration is straight from the Cockcroft Report (1982) and it is simply this: to achieve Grade 4 in CSE mathematics (representing the average level of attainment across the country) entails *failing* 70 per cent of the examination.

Curriculum change at Peers and new external initiatives

This background is important to an understanding of how change came about at Peers. New methods of delivering the curriculum could only follow a structural reorganisation of the school which got away from the practice of 20 or more departments working independently, to the idea of teams of teachers working together in more broadly-based curriculum areas. Other structural changes, such as blocking the timetable and reorganising the school day, encouraged this and out of the changes grew new ways of presenting the syllabus.

This background is also essential to understanding Peers' approach to the many curriculum initiatives coming from the outside such as the Lower Attaining Pupils Programme (LAPP) and the Technical and Vocational Education Initiative (TVEI). Significantly, because the change towards a modular curriculum, and the thinking and planning to organise this, came before these two (and also OCEA – Oxford Certificate of Educational Achievement – CPVE and GCSE), the new initiatives have been built into an existing structure for change and development rather than themselves being the mechanism for change. They have always adapted to follow the direction in which the school is moving as a whole, rather than being bolted onto an existing structure.

However, these initiatives *have* helped to bring about change – through extra staffing, new resources, links with outside bodies and so on – even if they have not determined it. They have also been important in giving formal recognition and validity to a system which might otherwise have seemed merely eccentric.

To illustrate this we can look at the school's response to Oxfordshire's involvement in the Lower Attaining Pupils Programmes, called New Learning Initiative (NLI) locally. Although there were certain strict criteria as regards the students who could benefit directly from the funds available through the project (the so-called bottom 40 per cent) the temptation to create a discrete NLI group was strongly resisted. Put another way, the school did not want to establish a new subject territory on the curriculum but rather to use an outside initiative to enhance what was already on offer with specific reference to the target group (the school's *entire* 40 per cent target group) within the school curriculum as a whole. It is interesting that, of the three strands to NLI in Oxfordshire, the one which initially could be offered only to an *artificially created discrete* group of students – Instrumental Enrichment – was therefore the least appropriate at Peers, while the other two, community linking and residential education, have noticeably influenced the school's thinking with benefits to all students. Community projects, a choice now fully available through the community studies modular arrangement (and very popular), grew directly out of the NLI while the belief that outdoor and residential experience should be an integrated part of the school diet for *all* students has stimulated progress here.

Other examples are the TVEI and OCEA. The TVEI modules, taken by 20 per cent of pupils, form part of the overall modular framework for all students. This makes it easier to extend the benefits of TVEI funding to other pupils in indirect ways. Equally, as a widely recognised Record of Achievement, OCEA can record on paper the many processes, like pupils' influence over their own curriculum, that underpin the success of the new Peers curriculum. All students have left in 1987 with an OCEA folder; wide educational experience is valued.

Thus during the last five years a curriculum strategy has been developed 'to broaden the basis upon which achievements in school could be recognised' (Moon and Oliver, 1985), aimed at improving school for all students. This has been accompanied by an ethos and practice in which teachers are actively encouraged to work in new ways, develop new skills and be more imaginative in their thinking about what constitutes success. In such a context, whole school responsibility for students with special educational needs follows naturally. The search for new ways to record achievement has opened up new areas for students to experience success and to learn in. Outdoor and residential education, community projects, the development of a maths curriculum based on problem-solving themes and activities have been natural outcomes. In addition, new initiatives in sport, and education for health and fitness combine well with the school's developing role as a community school with a sports and arts centre as well as a further education centre. A common feature of all these initiatives has been an extensive programme of secondments and in-service training enabling teachers in different sectors of the education service to meet, share and reflect upon their experiences.

Issues in relation to special needs

Implicit in the philosophy and rationale for the recent changes has been a belief that it is the school's responsibility to create the opportunities for its students to experience success, to be valued for what they are and to develop their full potential. Learning *difficulties* are not, then, the first focus of attention: learning *successes* are. In practice, this means that there is no crying demand for the withdrawal from modules of those students who would unquestionably have dropped out of a large proportion of two-year options. Nor is there any need for a 'sink group' to follow an alternative curriculum.

The flexibility of the modular curriculum enables curriculum packages to be suited to students requiring widely different pathways to achieve success. These packages can take into account the sometimes very specific needs, abilities and learning styles of individuals. In such a climate, 'having special needs' is not seen as a blanket term encompassing a group of students who are then collectively stigmatised; no pupils have statements under the 1981 Act. All students are encouraged, through self assessment, to construct their own targets and take responsibility with their teachers for meeting these and to review, evaluate and be proud of their achievements.

This presupposes an emphasis on equality, on determination to reduce unfair discrimination, on mutual respect between staff and students and high expectations. In order to underline and enhance the personal search for excellence there has also been a tradition of encouraging *all* members of the school community to share their interest and talents. The caretaker, as an amateur astronomer, has helped to run a course on astronomy and the school has appointed staff who have something to offer outside their teaching brief but who, above all, like teenagers.

Accordingly, the special needs department has become an integral resource for the school rather than an extension to it. It can, and does, support the operation of modules (and other aspects of school life) as well as run short term units of work alongside them but within the same framework. But at no point is any student the property of the special needs department. The answer to the question: 'Is he or she one of yours?' is: 'We don't have any'.

Evaluation

How successful have the changes been and how does one evaluate change on this scale? Numbers on roll? Exam results? Range of subjects followed? Number of students going on to full time employment and/or education? Number of suspensions? Does the fact that the school has twice won the School Curriculum Award (in 1984 and 1987) and has a regular stream of visitors from all over the country constitute success? It is very difficult to find suitable (and objective) criteria, although an impending full inspection by HMI may perhaps suggest some methods for achieving this. Some statistics may help, however, bearing in mind that a change which grew out of a challenge to an academic curriculum for all will be judged by the highest *academic* criteria. On completion of first cycle, 1986:

- The number of students leaving with *no* exam passes has been *halved*.
- In science/technology, the number of exam passes has increased by over 50 per cent over the previous year. Average grades achieved at the top end have improved by a half grade – the bottom end by $1\frac{1}{2}$ grades.
- In humanities, the number of exam passes has increased by over 50 per cent.

To be successful, however, an evaluation should indicate the problems to be faced and which remain to be solved. It is likely that these will mainly be to do with coordination, continuity and consolidation. Collaborative learning methods and new courses (particularly where there is not yet enough choice) need to be developed further. A successful evaluation will take into account the reactions of staff, pupils and parents, none of which is easy to gauge. Students have little comparative experience of schools; and parents and teachers with memories of their own schooling, now rapidly outdating, tend to range from the pleased or puzzled to the compliant. The knowledge, however, that the school's innovations have been, so to speak, endorsed by public awards, by its students' wide range of achievements and by the fact that so much of what once seemed innovative is now becoming commonplace, means that the local community is highly supportive.

Conclusion

There is a long way to go. Not only do the quality and range of the service constantly need to be improved (the hallmark of such a flexible system is that improvement is not only possible but imperative). If a system is to continue to be student-centred, it must also continue to adapt to new generations of students and the conditions in which they live. Once the door is closed for good on the notion that having special needs marks you out for separate treatment from the rest, the progress is open-ended. Let us only hope that the national curriculum door doesn't swing shut on it – in all our faces.

[This article was first published in *British Journal of Special Education* Vol. 14, No. 4, December 1987.]

References

ACE (1963) *Half Our Future* (Newsom Report). London: DES.

Department of Education and Science (1988) *Mathematics Counts* (The Cockcroft Report). London: HMSO (para.444).

Moon, R. and Oliver, L. (1985) 'Redefining school concepts of ability – the experience of the LAPP project'. *Curriculum*, 6, 3.

CHAPTER 6

Changing Direction at Tile Hill Wood

Carol Giles and Scott Dunlop

The Warnock Report (DES, 1978) and the 1981 Education Act both widen the concept of special educational need to include many children who do not have clearly identifiable physical, mental or sensory handicap. Both point clearly to the ordinary schools' responsibility to meet these pupils' special educational needs.

Traditionally in secondary schools these pupils' special needs have been thought of as the sole responsibility of the remedial department. Such departments often function in a similar fashion to a subject department and pupils attend them for a number of periods each week for small group teaching, principally in reading and spelling. This is the withdrawal approach. The remedial teacher is seen as an expert or specialist in teaching dull children to read and write and thus equipping them with the basic skills with which to cope with the curriculum offered by the subject department. Remedial departments which operate in a subject department role tend to be seen as the school's 'casualty service' in terms of its clientele (Lewis, 1984) and also tend to have low status and morale. Moreover it is highly questionable whether such remedial departments can give adequate help to the estimated 18 per cent of children with special educational needs in the ordinary schools. Pupils' special needs do not disappear when they leave the confines of the remedial department.

The need for a wider role for remedial departments and remedial teachers (NARE, 1979) is self evident and many secondary schools have attempted to meet their responsibilities to pupils with special needs in various fashions. This account reports the attempt of one

Coventry comprehensive school to review its own provision for pupils with special educational needs in the light of the 1981 Education Act and to respond to the challenge of developing a system which would ensure that all pupils received an education appropriate to their needs, for all of the week, and across the whole curriculum. It is not the intention here to argue the theoretical or indeed ideological justification for a whole school approach (many of the issues concerning special educational needs and the comprehensive principle are addressed by Quicke, 1981). This account outlines the practicalities in developing and implementing a whole school approach to meeting special needs in a girls' comprehensive school which is committed to mixed ability teaching and includes some pupils with moderate learning difficulties and several pupils with moderately impaired hearing and vision.

What's in a name? The coordinator for special needs

The retirement of the previous head of the remedial department provided a natural watershed and an opportunity for the school to develop in new directions. Three issues were seen to be of considerable importance: the name of the person 'in charge', the status of this person and the geographical location of the person/department. Of these three the choice of the name was possibly the most crucial.

The choice of title, 'coordinator for special needs', in preference to 'head of remedial department' was deliberate, because the intention was for every teacher within the school to take responsibility for meeting the special needs of pupils that they taught. It was essential to move away from the traditional idea of a remedial department staffed by teachers who had special skills and who employed methods unavailable to the subject teacher – the 'wonder teacher' (so vividly described by Lamont, 1981) with skills comparable only to those of Wonder Woman. To 'coordinate' means to get people or things working properly together, and this succinctly defines the role that the coordinator for special needs must play in a comprehensive school. Her main expertise must lie not in the application of esoteric teaching techniques but in the deployment of staff and resource management skills.

The status of the coordinator

For the coordinator to adopt a wider role than a head of a traditional remedial department and to enable her to promote a whole school approach to meeting special needs she has to be effective in influencing policy and organisation in the school. In short she has to have high status within the school. To help achieve this status the appointment of coordinator was made at scale IV level and she was made a member of both the academic and pastoral management teams as of right. Carrying out this wider role requires the coordinator to walk a diplomatic tightrope (Lewis, 1984), being forceful enough to influence decision making but remaining acceptable to all staff, from the newly appointed probationer upwards, in order to have access to their classrooms to fulfil the support teacher role and to sample the education being offered to the pupils.

The resource room – not the Porta-kabin model

A person's status is a product not only of her title, money and the company she keeps, but where she lives. The head of the remedial department traditionally resides in some half forgotten corner of the school often in a temporary building in the corner of the school playground (the Porta-kabin model of special needs provision). This was exactly the provision at Tile Hill Wood before the appointment of the coordinator. One of the first decisions was to emphasise the centrality of the coordinator's role by situating the coordinator's base (resource room) in one of the main teaching blocks. The room has no formal title and is simply known to staff and pupils as Mrs Giles' room – a small step in the delabelling process.

The necessity of planning a whole school approach

A whole school approach does not just happen; the whole school has to plan for it. At Tile Hill Wood the shape that special needs provision was to take was worked out over a school year by a working party which included senior staff and representatives from each subject area and also the pastoral staff. Since the eventual structures had to be acceptable to all staff it was essential to involve representatives from all areas at the outset.

These representatives were responsible for the flow of information to and from the working party to subject colleagues throughout the planning stages. Information was collected initially via a questionnaire to all departments. This was designed to elicit an overview of the existing provision for pupils with special needs within the school, together with suggestions for the shape of future provision. The exercise resulted in the role of the special needs department being defined as 'to promote and service a whole school approach to meeting the individual special needs of pupils wherever they are placed within the school'. A wide definition of the term 'special needs' was agreed upon to include pupils with specific learning difficulties, both long and short term, pupils with more general learning difficulties which affect their performance in most areas of the curriculum, pupils with physical difficulties such as hearing or vision impairment and pupils with emotional problems which affect their classroom behaviour and/or performance. The issue of so called disruptive pupils is a special case which is discussed later.

Figure 6.1 Functions and responsibilities of the coordinator for special needs

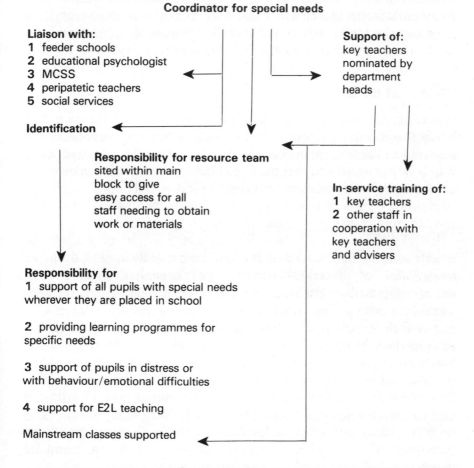

Once the structures for meeting special needs had been worked out by the working party the whole staff were taken through a discussion of the model (see Figure 6.1) at a staff meeting. They then voted, and accepted this as a way in which special needs would be organised at Tile Hill Wood School in the future.

This programme of consultation was considered to be central to the development of a whole school approach. McCall (1982) comments: 'Remedial education is both a horizontal and a vertical concept. Children carry their problems across the curriculum and long term benefits can only be achieved within the context of genuine team effort and cooperation'. It was important that the whole staff should have the opportunity to contribute to the discussion both within and across departments and then should do so through their individual vote, making a firm commitment to support a system which would affect every individual teacher in their own classroom. That no one voted against the proposed system was felt to be due to the presence of representatives of all interested groups in the school on the working party.

The role of the key teacher

It was agreed that each subject department would nominate a 'key teacher' who would be responsible for liaison between the coordinator and subject department colleagues. To ensure that the special needs of pupils were known and met the coordinator undertook to coordinate the work of the key teachers in respect of individual pupils' needs and to organise regular meetings and in-service training sessions for the key teachers to increase their understanding of special needs.

Initially the key teachers expressed concern that they might be unable to fulfil their new role but confidence rapidly increased when a programme of in-service training was organised around their perceived immediate needs. This programme is ongoing and includes workshops which focus on adapting curricular materials for use by pupils with specific needs in subject classrooms, talks by specialists such as the educational psychologist, school doctor, teachers of the hearing or visually impaired, discussion sessions on reading difficulties, spelling and working together with case studies of individual pupils. The role of these sessions is primarily to encourage positive attitudes and to help teachers to realise they already have many of the skills necessary to teach 'special needs children'. Topics discussed in sessions have included the marking of spelling mistakes in written work and the preparation of specialised spelling lists for subject areas.

Support service – the special needs telephone

The staff as a whole agreed that the coordinator should coordinate the work of all support agencies who come into contact with the school. These include the school psychological service, social services, minority group support service, peripatetic teachers concerned with specific handicaps and home tutors. This has resulted in a much more efficient service for the school and also for the support services since, through clarification of the pathways for communication, there is now less chance of confusion.

The system is well used because it is clearly defined and easily understood by all. It might be thought that such a system would cause conflict with the role of the pastoral care heads and tutors. In the event this has not happened because frequently the coordinator acts mainly as a clearing house for such communications and does not necessarily have to be the central figure in dealing with problems.

This form of organisation does, however, have implications for the organising abilities of the coordinator who must ensure that all communications are promptly relayed to the correct person and that no misunderstandings arise. Invaluable to the system has been the installation of an outside telephone, completely separate from the school switchboard. The number of this telephone has been given to the support agencies and to the parents of pupils with special needs and this minimises frustrating delays caused by a busy school switchboard. The 'special needs telephone' is a way by which parents can establish confidence in the coordinator, be assured of confidentiality and overcome the formality of telephoning a large organisation, which a comprehensive school is.

The role of the educational psychologist

When the coordinator for special needs took up post one of her first steps was to negotiate a method of working with the educational psychologist for the school. Both agreed that it was essential that they shared the same model of how the school was to meet special educational needs. Reeve (1980) argues that schools can have psychologists inside schools, working with the teachers in solving problems, or outside trying but not really solving these problems. Significantly, Reeve says 'the choice must be the teacher's', that psychologists and teachers can work together effectively only if they share a common perspective.

At Tile Hill Wood there were no significant problems. Just as the coordinator rejected the casualty service role, the psychologist wished to avoid the role of 'gatekeeper for special education' (Sheppard, 1978). Both psychologist and special needs coordinator saw pupils' special educational needs as much a function of the education the pupils were receiving as of any intrinsic deficit in the pupils themselves or in their families. The agreed way of working that was arrived at was that of the consultative model.

The school psychologist visits once a fortnight as a consultant and spends about the same amount of time again on individually arranged visits to meet children and parents. This can be seen as an example of a 'newer' way of working by educational psychologists and is not always readily acceptable by schools. Topping (1978) reported that, in one area of an English city where the psychologist worked in a consultative fashion, the headteachers indicated support for his way of working but also wanted individual casework.

There have been few problems at Tile Hill Wood since the psychologist adopted a consultative role primarily because of the care taken by the coordinator to communicate the psychologist's comments and advice to all the relevant teachers. However the consultative approach does not mean a distancing of the class teacher from the psychologist. Indeed there is now more contact between the psychologist and teachers during consultative visits than when the educational psychologist worked previously on a referral only basis. From time to time the psychologist may meet with all the teachers (12 or so) who teach a particular girl and work out strategies or approaches with them to meet her individual needs. To be effective the actual work of an educational psychologist must arise from discussion and planning with colleagues within the school (Jones and Jones, 1983).

There are two aspects of the consultative model that are not always appreciated. Firstly a consultative model does not imply that the psychologist does not see individual pupils (Burden, 1978). Properly understood a consultative approach has a selection function and ensures that the individual children whom the psychologist sees are the most appropriate and that those more suitable for other agencies (such as social services) are generally directed to them.

Secondly the consultative model does not imply an expert/client relationship between psychologist and school. The regular pattern of visiting has helped the educational psychologist to be seen as a colleague with somewhat different skills and perspectives who can be part of the whole school approach to special needs rather than an outside addition to the school's system. Two school projects where the psychologist has been used in an advisory role have been the experimental use of Data-Pac (primary materials) in reading, spelling and maths with secondary school children and a weekly social skills group for withdrawn and socially ineffective girls in their third year. The staff are currently awaiting the resolution of the teachers' action to embark upon an in-service course for meeting the needs of disruptive pupils based on *Preventive Approaches to Disruption* (Chisholm *et al.*, 1986).

Assessment of individual needs

The first of the roles of remedial teacher identified by NARE (1979) was assessment. However the assessment process as followed at Tile Hill Wood is far removed from a traditional practice of screening by normative tests of basic literacy skills. It starts before the pupil arrives at Tile Hill Wood and continues throughout her school career. Assessment is an ongoing process of measuring the pupil's response to the education she receives, not something that can be achieved by any test, normative or otherwise. Information about the needs of individual pupils is gathered before their arrival at the comprehensive school by meetings with feeder primary school headteachers and class teachers, observation of and discussion with the pupils, and contact with relevant support agencies and the pupils' parents. It is particularly useful that the school psychologist is also the psychologist for the feeder primary schools. Assessment of needs continues on a formal basis during the first two weeks of the autumn term (this may include some formal testing but certainly not always) and then throughout the pupil's school career by means of the key teachers' reports to and discussions with the special needs coordinator.

The role of the support teachers

Once needs have been assessed support staff are deployed within subject classrooms, as far as possible, to meet these needs. This is the main way of providing support. The school is organised on mixed ability teaching lines and the aim is to keep withdrawal to a minimum whilst accepting that it may be necessary to withdraw some pupils at some time if this is judged to be the most effective way to meet their needs. The keynote is flexibility and the aim is that staff should work alongside pupils as dictated by their individual need rather than the timetable dictating which need can be met.

The support staff are subject teachers, mainly but not exclusively key teachers. They opt to spend one or two lessons each week acting as special needs support teachers. The coordinator is responsible for allocating them to classrooms according to pupil need and teacher preference – it is interesting to note that the majority of support teachers opt to move outside their own subject department in an attempt to increase their knowledge of other subject areas. Informal training for support teachers takes the form of an initial individual discussion on their role, with the coordinator, during which information is given on specific children they are to support and specific tasks they are to carry out. As the support teacher role has been developed at Tile Hill during the long period of industrial action formal in-service training has been negligible. Much informal guidance is given by the coordinator on request from the support teacher and/or class teacher as the need arises.

In 1984–85, the first year of operation, 16 staff spent at least one lesson each week working as a special needs support teacher. (It is our eventual aim that *all* staff should have spent some time working as a special needs support teacher during their time in the school.) Staff requested that the role of the support teacher in relation to the class teacher be made explicit to avoid potential misunderstanding.

A formal document is therefore given to both teachers before they begin to work together. The role of the class teacher is defined as including the preparation of the lesson for the whole class, taking major responsibility for discipline, ensuring that lessons are planned and conducted so that pupils can extract maximum benefit from the presence of two teachers in the room. The support teacher works with specific pupils identified by the coordinator and any pupils identified as having special needs by the class teacher and prepares resources to meet specific needs. The support teacher must attend every lesson to ensure continuity of relationships with the group, even if a particular lesson is given over to watching television or drama. Support teachers never cover for the absence of the class teacher, a cover teacher is always provided.

Discussion outlines which examined areas of potential conflict were also prepared. Teachers who were to work together examined these outlines before embarking on this new, to most, experience of collaborative teaching. This increased confidence and decreased the possibility of uncomfortable or embarrassing situations arising in the classroom.

Special needs and the problem of disruption

In a comprehensive school there can be no fixed demarcation between academic and pastoral responsibilities. Neither can there be any clear distinction between pupils with special educational needs and those who present teachers with severe problems of discipline and control. In practice this means a considerable overlap of role between the co-ordinator and pastoral staff and, with this, potential for conflict between them. This overlap has often resulted in the practice of traditional remedial departments becoming 'dumping grounds' for disruptive pupils.

To help avoid possibilities of role overlap and illegitimate use of the coordinator's resource room, explicit guidelines for the role of the coordinator and procedures for dealing with disturbed and disruptive pupils were drawn up and negotiated with the entire staff. The basic approach adopted was that 'we are all in it together' and definite steps were taken to ensure that at all times the responsibility for the education of the disruptive pupil remained with the subject department involved. The coordinator for her part undertook to keep pastoral staff fully informed of the counselling and support contact she inevitably would have with pupils who were presenting behavioural problems to staff.

Evaluation

An essential part of the initiative is that its progress is monitored and to ensure that the initial impetus was not lost an evaluation session was held at the end of the first year. This indicated that pupils had benefited from help which was immediate and relevant to the task in hand. Pupils were receiving specific help and the number of self referrals for help had dramatically increased. Positive relationships developed as pupils realised the support teacher was there to help everyone and not only those pupils generally recognised as having learning difficulties.

The support teachers reported considerable satisfaction from monitoring individual pupils' progress and felt they had transferred their newly acquired skills developed with pupils with learning difficulties to their own subject classes. Subject teachers became quickly confident in having a support teacher working in their class-room – a potential area of difficulty as teachers are traditionally autonomous in their own classroom and tend to be wary of the presence of another teacher. Confidence perhaps developed because the support teacher was seen to be offering help which was practical and immediately relevant. Subject teachers also expressed pleasure that such an arrangement released some time each lesson for them to spend with pupils who might need to be academically stretched but who, through pressure of other demands in the classroom, were normally left to work independently.

Conclusion

It is still early days in the development of the whole school approach at Tile Hill Wood. However, cautious optimism can be expressed at progress so far. This form of organisation seems to have had a marked effect upon developing positive staff attitudes towards pupils with special needs and thus the idea that individual special needs can be met within normal subject classrooms. A direct result of support teachers working in classrooms has been the development of collaborative teaching skills. Interchanges of information between curriculum areas and curriculum development work have been possible. All of this benefits the *total* school population, not only pupils with special needs. Our experiences would seem to be powerful evidence for a move away from the traditional role of the remedial department towards a co-ordinated whole school approach. Such benefits can be achieved, however, only if the entire staff understand and accept the special needs policy of the school. This requires consultations and discussions which involve the whole school, such as happened at Tile Hill Wood. The coordinator herself could not have achieved this nor managed a highly complex role without the support given by senior school staff and LEA advisers.

[This article was first published in *British Journal of Special Education* Volume 13, No. 3: September 1986.]

References

Burden, R. (1978) 'Schools' System Analysis: a Project-centred Approach'. In Gillham, W. E. C. (ed.) *Reconstructing Educational Psychology.* London: Croom Helm.

Chisholm, B., Tearney, D., Knight, G., Little, H., Morris, S. and Tweddle, D. (1986) *Preventive Approaches to Disruption. Developing Teaching Skills.* London: Macmillan.

Department of Education and Science (1978) *Special Educational Needs* (Warnock Report). London: HMSO.

Jones, N. J., and Jones, E. M. (1983) 'Psychological services in the Banbury project'. *Journal of the Association of Educational Psychologists*, **6**, 2: 41–44.

Lamont, C. (1981) 'Strategies for in-school development'. *Newsletter of the Scottish Association for Remedial Education*, **24**: 6–9.

Lewis, G. (1984) 'A supportive role at secondary level.' *Remedial Education*, **19**, 1: 1–12.

McCall, C. (1982) 'Some recent national reports and surveys: implications for the remedial specialist'. In Hinson, M., Hughes, M. (eds.) *Planning Effective Progress*. Amersham: Hulton/NARE.

National Association for Remedial Education (1979) *The Role of Remedial Teachers*. Guidelines No. 2. Stafford: NARE.

Quicke, J. (1981) 'Special educational needs and the comprehensive principle. Some implications of ideological critique'. *Remedial Education*, **16**, 2: 61–65.

Reeve, C. J. (1980) 'The educational psychologist and children with learning difficulties'. In Raybould, E. C., Roberts, B., and Wedell, K. (eds.) *Helping the Low Achiever in the Secondary School*. Birmingham University Educational Review. Occasional Publications No. 7.

Sheppard, J. (1978) 'The educational psychologist as special school gatekeeper'. *Journal of the Association of Educational Psychologists*, **4**, 9: 21–24.

Topping, K. J. (1978) 'Consumer confusion and professional conflict in educational psychology'. *Bulletin of the British Psychological Society*, **31**: 265–267.

CHAPTER 7

Developing a Network of Support

Margaret Buck

What is support?

The term 'support' defies simplistic definitions and this fact emphasises the complex inter-relationship between the purposes and targets of support. Hockley (1985) suggests that the short term emphasis of support should be on helping individual students and on advising staff how to manage students, whilst the long term emphasis should be on extending the skills and expertise of class teachers. As Edwards (1985) points out with some logic:

> The most effective approach is to support staff because it is quite impossible for a special needs department to provide the assistance required by every pupil in every other department.

Lewis (1984), offering a 'support service' to all students, irrespective of their academic ability, and to all teachers, to encourage them to accept responsibility for all students' learning needs, seems to recognise the complementary need for both kinds of support so that:

> a professional dialogue can be established encouraging a joint development and partnership in subject planning, teaching and curriculum.

which would seem compatible with the rationale of a whole school response.

Hart (1986) suggests that inherent in the nature of support teaching there needs to be an element of prevention as well as intervention. Defining special needs as relative to a school's ability to provide for individual differences, as opposed to something that students 'have', Hart argues that the support teacher's role needs to include preventive responsibilities involving the teacher in curriculum review, planning and design.

Tile Hill Wood School embarked on initiating and implementing a whole school response to students' individual needs in 1982 (Giles and Dunlop, 1986). During the last seven years the evolutionary nature of the development of the model has emphasised the fundamental necessity for the support network to be dynamic and constantly subject to evaluation.

Tile Hill Wood's experiences suggest that support should be directed to students, to teachers and the curriculum (Buck, 1987). Support is more than 'in-class support'; it constitutes the complex network of responses which a school makes in its attempts to meet all students' needs. Tile Hill Wood's view of support springs from a philosophical approach which, rather than viewing a few students as having special needs, sees all students as having individual needs. The model of provision depends on a philosophy, not a departmental structure; therefore it lacks the visible features of a department. There is no syllabus for students with 'special needs', no departmental identity, no specialist staff apart from the coordinator for special needs. This is quite deliberate. There are no special classes for special students taught by specialist teachers: all teachers share the task of meeting the needs of all the students and subject departments are responsible for making the curriculum accessible to all.

Figure 7.1 Purposes of support

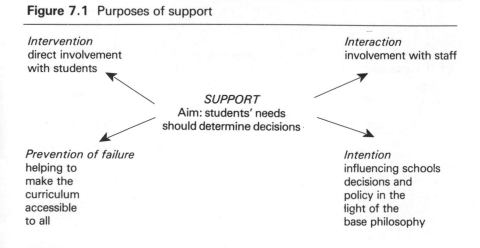

In a whole school response decisions about support should be determined by students' needs; students should not be selected in order to fill the pre-determined available provision. This 'needs-led' rather than 'provision-led' approach suggests that the purposes of support need to be closely examined. Figure 7.1 suggests that four purposes of support can be made explicit.

Who supports?

Acceptance that in-class support is but one dimension of a broader concept of support means that offering 'support' is not exclusive to support teachers. Support to students is offered by *all* staff. At Tile Hill Wood, a school committed to a philosophy of mixed ability teaching, all the members of staff are committed to meeting the needs of all the students with whom they come in contact.

Figure 7.2 A support network

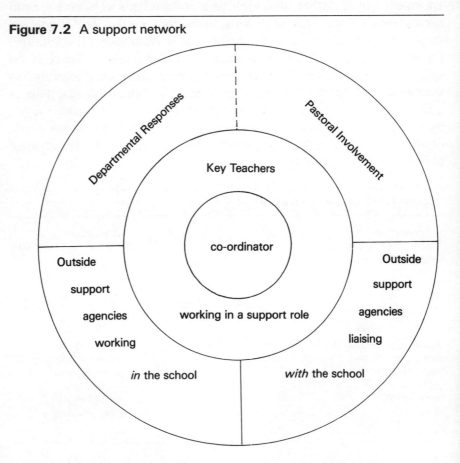

Support, construed as intervention, interaction, prevention and intention, is the aim of the network of support operating within the school. The coordinator's responsibility is to develop and coordinate the support network, which is part of whole school response, and to work through the 'key teachers' and the departmental and pastoral responses within the school. (Every department has a 'key teacher' who promotes liaison between the department and the coordinator.) It would be counter-productive if the coordinator's involvement or the organisation of support reduced the level of responsibility that members of staff feel for students in their care.

Support is also offered by outside agencies such as the schools' psychological service, child guidance, the service for the hearing impaired, the service for the visually impaired, the special programme team for disruptive students, the minority group support service for students if English is their second language, the school health services, social services and so on (Giles and Dunlop, 1986). The outside services can offer direct help by working in the school or indirect help by liaising with the school. (See Figure 7.2)

Stages in developing a support network

Support as a concept and as a working practice cannot be introduced overnight to any school. At Tile Hill Wood the understanding of 'support' has clearly progressed in stages.

Stage 0: A philosophical base

If a school wishes to introduce 'support' it is advisable to begin with an appraisal of the philosophy upon which future decisions will be grounded. This process can be promoted in various ways: by setting up a working party; or by using other means, such as questionnaires, as was done at Tile Hill Wood (Giles and Dunlop, 1986).

Having decided on its base philosophy and its thinking about 'special needs', the school can then interpret what the term 'support' means in the context of the school community. The philosophy of the school will be the touchstone for any decisions; it will generate the structures of response to students' needs; it will give unity to the organisation within the school rather than allowing 'support' to become a 'bolt-on' initiative.

The Tile Hill Wood philosophy is that of a whole school response with every teacher sharing the responsibility for meeting each student's individual needs.

Stage 1: Initial deployment of support

Initially the coordinator (at that time Carol Giles) was the only member of staff offering individual support, in-class support and support to groups of students withdrawn from mainstream lessons. The main subject areas were English, mathematics and the first year course of integrated English and humanities. Some support was offered by the outside support services as deemed appropriate to meet the needs of individual students.

At this stage the key teachers were the link between their departments and the coordinator, making possible a two-way flow of information about students' needs. The key teachers were also encouraged to act as first-line advisers to their departmental colleagues on matters such as the preparation of resources and appropriate strategies for meeting students' needs.

Stage 2: Support is extended

At this stage the coordinator continued to offer individual support, in-class support and support to groups of students withdrawn from mainstream lessons, mainly English, mathematics and the first year course of integrated English and humanities. The key teachers continued their liaison work and some offered advice to their departmental colleagues. In addition help was offered by 'support teachers'.

The support teachers were mainstream staff drawn from various subject areas, including art, history and religious education, most of whom had volunteered to work with students who had particular needs. These teachers were engaged in individual, group or in-class support mainly in English and mathematics or integrated English and humanities. The outside support services continued to offer support to individual students as in the past.

Stage 3: New models

Continual evaluation is a necessary part of Tile Hill Wood's approach to meeting students' individual needs and the school has also undergone a curriculum review in the last two years. The nature of support has changed somewhat and reflects feedback from question-naires and discussions with the personnel involved.

The coordinator continues to offer individual, group and in-class support but students are now withdrawn from mainstream lessons only on a temporary basis; usually it is left to the student(s) to decide the context of the support. The coordinator continues to support in integrated English and humanities, English and mathematics but has extended into other areas of the curriculum. As before, the outside support services continue to offer support to individual students as necessary.

Two new initiatives have been introduced. Firstly, the key teachers are now operating as support teachers to their own departments for at least one double period a week. This means that, unlike in the past, the key teacher has the opportunity to act as a support teacher and gain experience in the role. Secondly, almost all teachers in the English and mathematics departments are presently timetabled to offer one lesson of support to their own departments. These initiatives seem to have been well received and are currently subject to evaluation.

One problem that has arisen is that staff would now like even more timetabled support from their departmental colleagues. Interestingly, teachers who have been giving support have spoken of their increased awareness of students' needs and of related issues such as the importance of making the curriculum more accessible.

The experience of 'support' can generate a positive working relationship between two members of staff and therefore staff may actively seek to work in a support relationship. It is vital, therefore, that there is a professional commitment to use the resource of 'support' in the best way possible.

Developing support

If 'support' is going to be successful, whether it is teachers working together in the classroom or resourcing the curriculum, or liaising to discuss the needs of an individual or a group, there has to be a recognition of the professional partnership involved. Central to the whole process is the establishment of a comfortable working relation-ship.

Support can benefit students, teachers and the curriculum, and it can influence the mode of curriculum delivery. But such benefits will not automatically happen just because two teachers are timetabled together and have the opportunity to work in the same classroom.

Both must work at developing a personal and professional relationship which makes the most of the resource of an extra teacher and addresses the purposes of the provision. Tile Hill Wood's experiences emphasise the need for the support teacher to be a willing volunteer and for the class teacher to be positive about the arrangement. Both must be committed to making support work in order to overcome difficulties relating to liaison, planning and preparation.

There can be no hard and fast rules about the support relationship; individuals will obviously develop their own style of working together. However, there are certain common areas that staff need to discuss before they enter into the support relationship. It is useful to have a relatively formal document which raises certain issues which need to be discussed and which may be troubling certain teachers; it provides the context for staff to air their concerns and express their views without being threatening or 'personal'. There is a document offering support guidelines at Tile Hill Wood and in part it sets out an agenda for discussion between staff.

What support is *not*

There are accounts of experiences of support but there is not yet a body of theory. In a sense teachers' actual experiences of support are providing the basis for generating the theory, the expectations and the practice. Each teacher's experiences will determine his or her general understanding and personal construct of what support is, and in consequence the teacher's commitment, or lack of it. This situation indicates the need for teachers to share their experiences of support so that they can broaden and widen what otherwise might be a very restricted understanding gained in a limited context.

- Support must not involve teachers in strategies which disable students. Teachers should not collude with students to avoid the challenge of the curriculum. Support should not be reading the worksheets to students and telling them the answers; it should not prevent them from experiencing learning through interaction with their peers.
- Support must not disable teachers. It must not take away the mainstream teachers' responsibility to teach; it must not take away the opportunities for subject teachers to increase their knowledge and understanding about students' needs.
- Support must not maintain an alternative curriculum for a few.

Professionals must not see support teaching as another way of being a remedial teacher, offering a remedial curriculum via remedial approaches.

● Support must not maintain an inadequate or inaccessible curriculum because the support teacher interprets the worksheets the students cannot read, or the instructions they cannot understand or the tasks they cannot perform. Support must enable students to learn, teachers to teach and the curriculum to be accessible to all.

On reflection

Schools may set up structures which make a whole school response possible but this fact alone will not guarantee that individual needs are met. Schools must focus on the content, the delivery and the accessibility of the curriculum. There must be more and more emphasis on the crucial contribution of subject departments and the role of the subject teacher. Support arrangements should acknowledge this.

The fact that students carry their needs across the curriculum also emphasises the importance of having cross-curricular policies that relate to language, marking, multi-cultural issues, assessment and equal opportunities, to name but a few areas. Subject departments cannot remain isolated empires that fiercely guard their independence on matters of policy if the consequences disable students' learning. A support network can facilitate such 'whole school' developments.

Above all, it is important to acknowledge that what has happened at Tile Hill Wood over the last seven years and what will happen in the future depends on the support of the LEA advisers and the senior management of the school but, above all, the whole staff. It is the staff who must make real the basic act of faith that support *can* work. It is wise for the person who coordinates the support network of a whole school response to remember that he or she is 'just' the coordinator; the coordinator alone cannot move mountains. It is to the credit of the staff that they have made it possible for Tile Hill Wood to break out of the 'remedial department mould'. We hope circumstances will continue to encourage the staff to maintain the climate which makes it possible for this more flexible model of provision to continue to develop.

A whole school response is a very fragile thing; but fragile things are often very precious! . . . A whole school response may be fragile but it is of such potential value that schools wishing to implement this model should treat it with respect and care and encourage all members of staff to appreciate its precious quality (Buck, 1987).

References

Buck, M. (1987) 'An Evaluation of a Whole School Approach in a Secondary School'. M.Ed. dissertation, Birmingham University.

Edwards, C. (1985) 'On launching a support service'. *British Journal of Special Education*, **12**, 2: 53–55.

Hart, S. (1986) 'In-class support teaching: Tackling Fish'. *British Journal of Special Education*, **13**, 2: 57–59.

Hockley, L. (1985) 'On being a support teacher . . . ' *British Journal of Special Education*, **12**, 1: 27–29.

Giles, C. and Dunlop, S. (1986) 'Changing Direction at Tile Hill Wood'. *British Journal of Special Education*, **13**, 3: 120–123. See foregoing chapter.

Lewis, G. (1984) 'A supportive role at secondary level'. *Remedial Education*, **19**, 1: 1–12.

SECTION 2

Special Educational Needs in the Classroom

One of the ways in which the process of curriculum change discussed in Section 1 can go wrong is when participants who arc required to implement the new way of working feel unable to do so. As a result, innovation remains largely at the level of rhetoric-stated policies that are not reflected in actual practice.

This means that in the move towards a whole school approach to meeting special educational needs an important focus of attention must be directed towards the classroom. It is through the day-to-day interactions of teachers and their pupils that special needs may be avoided, created or met.

Consequently the chapters in this second section are concerned with the question: 'How can pupils' special educational needs be met in the ordinary classroom?' Much of the discussion is concerned with ways of using human and material resources to make the delivery of the curriculum more responsive to the needs of individual pupils.

In the first chapter Ann Hodgson uses data from a research project to look at the ways in which teachers organise their classrooms in order to facilitate learning with particular respect to those pupils who may experience difficulties. She focuses on three areas: preparing subject material, presenting it to pupils and interacting with pupils to aid their learning. Mel Ainscow's chapter is also about teaching and learning. His concern is with trying to understand what it is that successful teachers do that makes them successful.

One important strand in the development of whole school approaches to meeting special educational needs has been the introduction of support teaching. The topic remains a contentious one. Debate continues around issues such as the purpose of support teaching, who should do it, how it should be organised and whether or not it is a good use of human resources.

Lois Hockley's chapter addresses the topic from the point of view of a support teacher working in a number of schools. Jean Garnett looks more specifically at principles underlying the practice of classroom support, again emphasising the importance of this as a strategy for providing access to the curriculum.

In the final chapter in this section Margaret Buck continues the discussion she began in chapter 7 by describing in some detail models and strategies that can be used in supporting students, teachers and the curriculum.

Going through the chapters in this section on classroom practice the reader needs to be aware of a tension that exists just beneath the surface. It is concerned with whether the focus of attention should be on helping individual pupils to overcome difficulties they face or whether it is more appropriate to use available resources to develop forms of teaching that are likely to minimise the occurrence of such difficulties.

This is not an easy issue for practitioners to resolve, particularly as they come into contact daily with pupils who can be seen as victims of the limitations of our school system. A sensible compromise, as reflected in many of the strategies described in this section, is to use both orientations in a complementary fasion. It has to be said, however, that such a compromise is often difficult to achieve.

CHAPTER 8

Meeting Special Needs in Mainstream Classrooms

Ann Hodgson

The academic organisation of the school, the formal grouping of pupils, the curriculum content on offer, staffing level and expertise all have an effect on learning opportunities available to pupils with special educational needs. However, what matters in the end is how pupils are taught, whether in mainstream classes alongside peers or withdrawn from these classes for individual small group tuition. What happens inside the classroom affects pupils' learning most immediately and it is this element that is under the class teacher's control.

Teachers can promote learning within the classroom by appropriate classroom organisation, by what they teach and how they teach it. In this chapter we look at some of the ways teachers organise their teaching to take account of the mainstream setting. This has been broken down into three parts, corresponding to the main activities that teachers engage in: preparing subject material; presenting it to pupils; and interacting with pupils to aid their learning. The data comes from the National Foundation for Educational Research Project 'Meeting Special Educational Needs in the Ordinary School' (Hodgson *et al.*, 1984).

Preparation of materials

For some pupils with special needs, selection of material and preparation for a particular mode of presentation are major considerations which may necessitate additional material or subject modification. Often the additional work benefited other pupils in the group whose cognitive development was at a similar stage to that of the pupil with special needs or whose learning style was more attuned to the different presentation.

An initial task in preparing material was to identify the key concepts which had to be covered if pupils were to cope with topic areas. Many teachers recorded this kind of information in duplicated handouts to ensure that the concepts discussed in a lesson were grasped by pupils and retained accurately. Work cards and handouts for the class were sometimes adapted or accompanied by an additional sheet which gave simple explanations of key terms. For example, many pupils with moderate learning difficulties could tackle the work done by the rest of their class if it was prepared in a simple form and individualised instructions were available. Such pupils coped better with handouts prepared in print or capital letters rather than cursive writing. As well as the usual handouts and work cards prepared for the class, an additional sheet explaining key words at the pupil's level of understanding was found to be useful. A simple example of this technique is shown in this extract from a handout given to pupils with moderate learning difficulties participating in a mixed ability science lesson: ' . . . most materials expand (grow bigger) when heated and contract (grow smaller) when cooled . . . '

Step by step descriptions of how to perform experiments were also available to pupils with special needs at the same school. During practical lessons the pupils worked with peers of higher ability, and as well as their own work cards had access to textbooks used by the rest of the class. The work cards simplified the diagrams. They also included a list of items needed for the experiment and any safety rules relating to it. Having carried out the experiment, pupils wrote up what they did with the aid of an information card which specified the information that the teacher wanted the pupil to record accurately and a structure within which to record it.

Although this preparation cost the class teacher additional time and effort, the material accrued was found to be useful for other groups at the school such as hearing impaired pupils. A hearing impaired pupil, dependent on lipreading, cannot take notes *and* watch the teacher's lips, and will therefore benefit from a prepared handout summarising the lesson content. Also the reduced language experience of many hearing impaired pupils means that they have difficulties with syntax and may confuse the meaning of sentences. The simple explanations given in the work cards helped to ensure that they recorded work accurately.

A further level of preparation was necessary for visually impaired pupils who required enlarged print or braille materials. These had to be ordered well in advance and required teachers to plan the content of their lesson well ahead of time. This could give rise to over-preparation initially as many teachers remarked that, at the beginning, they felt everything they might need for the lesson had to be enlarged. As one teacher explained, until she received feedback from pupils she was never sure which of several texts she was going to require. She planned her programme on a weekly basis and gave everything that might need enlargement to the peripatetic teacher.

As teachers got to know their pupils, however, it became obvious that certain texts had a style appropriate to individual pupils' learning and teachers enlarged only those particular texts, without detriment to the lesson flow. For most schools such over-preparation was not wasted as they had a continuing intake of visually impaired pupils who could benefit from the additional material. The materials prepared by a class teacher were generally stored and kept accessible to other class teachers so that, as time went on, the need for new preparation was reduced.

For the blind pupil, or the partially sighted one who is a braille reader, appropriate braille texts and materials have to be acquired. As there is not a wealth of braille material available, teachers were generally restricted to the texts available. Sometimes brailling of specific texts for examination subjects was carried out. This could take considerable time so that long term planning was necessary.

As an alternative strategy, or when appropriate braille materials were not available, some class teachers prepared tapes of set books or dictated lesson notes for use by the blind pupil after the lesson. Such preparation was time-consuming, but a library of taped material could be built up and made available to other pupils whose learning style depended more on an auditory mode than a visual mode. The Royal National Institute for the Blind (RNIB) was found to be a useful source of taped books for blind pupils.

Many teachers commented that planning lessons for pupils with special needs in mind had forced them to think through the material more and to plan accordingly, to the benefit of all pupils in the class. Much of the material prepared was not pupil-specific and could be used for the benefit of other pupils. For example, a number of teachers found that models which had been prepared so that visually impaired pupils could handle them helped sighted pupils also to grasp abstract concepts more easily.

Presentation of materials

The presentation of learning materials to a group of pupils follows on from how it has been prepared. The inclusion of pupils with special needs in mainstream classes has forced many teachers to re-think their mode of presentation, a task which has benefited many other pupils, as their learning and grasp of topics were enhanced by a presentation style that was better structured and was more sensitive to pupil feedback. Where pupils had difficulties in learning, teachers found it advantageous to introduce topics in a slow step-by-step way, using concrete examples and objects wherever possible. Additional manipulative materials which had been afforded blind/partially sighted pupils were also found to benefit pupils with other learning difficulties.

Pupils with moderate learning difficulties can cope with much subject material, even at secondary stage, if it is presented at the concrete level. One secondary school found that many such pupils could work with the rest of the class when they were able to manipulate materials. For example, in science basic principles of electricity and electrical circuits were understood if pupils could handle concrete objects. They were also allowed to represent their experiments as drawings rather than in symbolic diagrams. When presented with the same material in the usual symbolic way, as in circuit diagrams, these pupils completely failed to grasp the concepts. Where it is not possible to present subject material in a three dimensional form, there may be scope to present visual material in an enlarged or simplified form.

It may be necessary to alter the focus of the material in order to get a particular concept over to a pupil. Certain visual concepts such as light, colour and reflection may have to be tackled in quite a different way for visually impaired pupils. The science teacher at one primary school planned some lessons on shadows, using heat lamps for the visually impaired pupils instead of lights.

Frequent repetition, gauged by feedback from pupils, was also necessary. A particular problem of presentation arises when pupils are being taught in mixed ability lessons. The degree of repetition or simplification of instructions necessary for the sake of one or two pupils may be counterproductive for the rest of the class. Some teachers coped with this situation by giving further help and explanation to those pupils who needed it immediately after whole class instruction.

Others found it helpful to break the class into groups of four to five and instructions given to the group as a whole were repeated and clarified within the groups for those pupils who needed it.

Teacher-pupil interaction

Teacher interaction with pupils to promote learning is a major component of the teaching process. This entails asking questions, promoting discussion and generally engaging in verbal interaction. We examined this in terms of the frequency with which such interaction took place, the comprehensibility of the language used and the nature of any reinforcement given.

The amount and frequency of interaction between teachers and pupils with special needs varied widely, not always in accordance with the latter's need of it. Many pupils with special needs benefited from more instructional time than their classmates whereas others with comparable needs received far less. The critical factor seemed to be teachers' awareness of individual pupils' need for additional guidance and explanation. When teachers were so aware, they were happy to spend further time with individuals as necessary.

Many pupils with special needs, however, are adept at appearing to understand and keeping a low profile. (An alternative tactic to mask a failure to understand is, of course, to engage in disruptive behaviour.) This seemed to be a regular feature of many classrooms observed in the course of our study. Hearing impaired pupils followed their peers keenly, raising their hands when they did and going along with activities without really understanding what they were doing; visually impaired pupils went to great lengths to conceal their difficulties, not acknowledging problems in reading from the board or from poorly duplicated sheets; generally, pupils with learning difficulties refrained from participating in class activities that might 'show them up'. Unfortunately, these low profile tactics seemed to work, particularly in large classes and with teachers who were not versed in special needs, and many pupils received less instructional time from teachers than they needed.

Just as written handouts and workcards need to be adapted to the learning needs of pupils, verbal interaction likewise should be adjusted by the teacher. Speech must obviously be related to pupils' level of language development, and a balance found between pupils' everyday language and any technical terms or formal discourse judged necessary. The type of questioning used is a further consideration.

Many teachers tended to use 'closed' questions (allowing for a single correct answer only), which had the effect of discouraging pupils from making all but the briefest of responses, when a more open-ended approach would encourage pupil verbalisation and enable the teacher to give more specific instruction.

Regular reinforcement is another feature of the teaching process which is no less important for pupils with special needs than for other pupils. Many indeed, particularly those with moderate learning difficulties, need extrinsic reinforcement in greater measure and for longer periods than their peers. Some teachers found this difficult, remarking on the seeming inability of pupils to work without constant reassurance that they were doing the right thing. This was not something they expected to have to provide, particularly at secondary level, and teachers needed to appreciate that, while pupils must develop independent working habits, some have to be weaned away from dependence on constant reassurance in a very slow and gradual way.

[This article was first published in *British Journal of Special Education* Volume 12, No. 3: September 1985.]

Reference

Hodgson, A., Clunies-Ross, L. and Hegarty, S. (1984) *Learning Together: Teaching Pupils with Special Educational Needs in the Ordinary School.* Windsor: NFER/Nelson.

CHAPTER 9

How Should We Respond to Individual Needs?

Mel Ainscow

The traditional response of the school system to children experiencing difficulty in learning was to assume that this was as a result of their limitations, disabilities or disadvantages. Learning difficulties were assumed to lie within children. Consequently the aim was to determine what was wrong with the child so as to decide what to do in order to improve the situation.

Increasingly in recent years the limitations of this approach have come to be recognised. First and foremost this has led to an understanding that assuming that learning difficulties rested within children tended to lead us to label some children as being different or special. The outcomes of this were that they were expected to achieve less and, as a result, were given less challenging tasks that emphasised the idea that they were inadequate. Frequently the tasks they were set required them to work alone, either within the class or in a separate area of the school. Consequently, as well as not experiencing the stimulation and challenge offered to the rest of the class, they were also disadvantaged by not having the support and encouragement of working collaboratively with their classmates.

The overall feature of so much of the traditional remedial response came to be one of narrowness of opportunity. In other words the curriculum offered to this group of children was both limited and limiting.

In recognition of this argument there have been moves in recent years to find new ways of responding to children experiencing difficulties in ordinary classrooms. Such moves assume that difficulties arise because of the interaction of a whole range of factors, some of which lie within children, others connected with decisions made by teachers. The recognition of this fact leads to an optimistic frame of mind. It reminds us that what teachers do, the decisions they make, the experiences they provide, and the relationships they have with their pupils, all have a major influence on children's learning.

This new thinking also takes account of the dangers associated with the idea of labelling. Instead of grouping children together because they are seen as being 'special' or 'remedial' it works from the assumption that all children are special. Consequently the aim must be to respond to all pupils as individuals, recognising individuality as something to be respected, even celebrated.

All of this means that instead of providing separate learning experiences for groups of special children, primary and secondary schools have to find ways of offering a curriculum that takes account of individual needs. In other words the aim must be to make all teaching more effective in order that all pupils can participate in, and have the advantage of, the same range of curriculum opportunities. This represents what has come to be called 'a whole school approach'.

This leads us, of course, to the central issue faced by all teachers: how can teaching be made more responsive to the needs of individual pupils?

In this chapter I propose to review some of the evidence that arises from research about teaching, particularly with respect to teachers who are effective in responding to individual needs within the curriculum, with a view to making some suggestions. I would hope that these could be used as a basis for discussions within schools as they attempt to develop policies for meeting special needs.

Classroom process

For many years my interest has been in finding out what it is that successful teachers do that makes them successful – successful, that is, in terms of meeting the individual needs of pupils in their classes. This has led me to reflect upon my own experiences as a teacher, trying to understand what I have learned from my own trial and error efforts. I have also had the privilege of watching many other teachers at work in their classrooms. My understanding of their work has been helped by reading around some of the research evidence about effective teaching (e.g. Mortimore *et al.*, 1986; Porter and Brophy, 1988; Walberg and Wang, 1987).

In making my suggestions therefore, I am drawing on these sources, outlining some of the strategies that successful teachers use in order to respond to the individual needs and, therefore, the special needs of pupils in their classes.

There are *three* aspects of teaching that seem to me to be essential to success. These are:

(1) Teachers have to know their pupils well in terms of their existing skills and knowledge, their interests, and their previous experience.
(2) Pupils have to be helped to establish a sense of personal meaning about the tasks and activities in which they are engaged.
(3) Classrooms have to be organised in ways that encourage involvement and effort.

In broad terms effective teachers achieve these aims by emphasising: purpose; variety and choice; reflection and review; flexible use of resources; and co-operative learning. I will now look at these issues in more detail.

Purpose

Whenever I observe children who are not getting on with their work in class I am almost always aware of their lack of understanding as to the purpose of what they have been asked to do. Invariably they will say, if asked, that they are doing something because they have been asked to do so by their teacher. Indeed I am quite often surprised at the willingness of so many children to continue trying hard to complete assignments that must seem pointless.

Learning is about finding personal meanings from experience (Wells, 1986). It requires us to understand what we are about and relate this to our existing knowledge and previous experience. Consequently, if we are unclear about the purpose of an activity, learning is less likely.

In my experience effective teachers stress meaning in their work. They find ways of helping their pupils understand the purposes of particular tasks, the reasons they have been set, how they are to be carried out and by when. As a result their pupils are able to take responsibility for their own learning and, therefore, work with a strong sense of purpose.

The question is, how do teachers help pupils to have a greater understanding of the nature and purposes of the tasks that are set? Different teachers have different strategies that seem to work for them in this respect. It is partly a matter of style and personal preference.

Some teachers, for example, prefer a fairly didactic approach, characterised by an emphasis on telling. The way in which they help their pupils to understand what is going on is by careful explanation and demonstration (Rosenshine, 1983). On the other hand, many teachers prefer a less directive style, seeking to encourage understanding by discussion and negotiation with their pupils (Ainscow and Tweddle, 1988).

There are advantages and disadvantages in either style. The more directive teacher tends to organise activities in ways that allow her time to talk to her pupils as a class or in groups. Consequently the time spent on verbal encounters that are focused on the content of a particular activity is relatively high. The problem may be that some members of the class will find her explanations difficult to follow. On the other hand, a less directive teacher may emphasise discussion with individuals or small groups as he moves around the room observing the pupils at work and intervening where necessary. This allows him the opportunity to pitch explanations at a level appropriate for particular pupils, and check understanding by informal questions. The obvious problem here is that with large classes it will take time to get around to all members of the class.

Accepting that individual differences of teaching style should exist, there is a good case for the use of a variety of approaches for emphasising meaning. At times the use of clear presentation to a whole class, perhaps supplemented by a demonstration, is a cost effective way of talking to children at a level that can inspire and stimulate their thinking, particularly where the topic under consideration lends itself to a formal explanation. When this approach is used, however, it is vital to check the children's understanding by questioning and asking individuals to outline what they have understood by what has been said (Rosenshine, 1983).

My experience is that this rather traditional approach of telling children and then checking understanding is very effective, even with quite young children. Sadly the emphasis that has been placed on more active approaches to learning in recent years has tended to give some teachers the impression that talking to the whole class is wrong!

Equally the work of the teacher whilst children are actively engaged in activities is critical to the encouragement of greater understanding (Brophy, 1983; Rosenshine, 1983). It is in the nature of some tasks that children get clear indications as to the success or otherwise of their efforts. For example, with certain motor tasks such as completing a jigsaw or catching a ball, children know how well they are performing although they may still need guidance as to how they might improve. With many classroom tasks, however, children may not know if they are on the right lines. Indeed they may carry on in an inappropriate way, possibly practising errors.

Effective teachers seem to find ways of keeping the whole class busy in order that they can engage individuals or small groups in detailed discussions about what they are doing and why (Kounin, 1970). Organisation of time and resources is obviously critical in this respect and I will return to this topic later.

Variety and choice

The audience in front of you is a captive one – they are required to be there. Nevertheless teaching is to some degree show business. Our task as teachers is in part, at least, to entertain. Whilst there is a need for challenge and pressure in order to motivate effort, a degree of audience appeal is also a necessary feature of effective teaching (Kounin, 1970).

We start out, of course, with some advantages. Most children are interested in learning. They want to find out more about the world. By and large they are also keen to please their teachers and gain the approval of their classmates. Our task is to mobilise their curiosity and desire for recognition, stimulate if, inform it and direct it towards topics and issues that are worthy of attention.

One of the keys to audience appeal in any setting, including classrooms, is variety. This means variety in terms of both what is done and how. So, effective teachers plan their lessons in order to offer their pupils a range of different topics and a variety of learning contexts within which to work (Ainscow and Muncey, 1989). They also look to offer variety through their use of diverse classroom materials.

Another important reason for emphasising variety is to do with the individual differences of pupils. Offering them the opportunity to take part in different types of learning encounter can help them to become more aware of themselves as learners. Our aim must be not only to teach our children interesting and useful facts and skills, but also to enable them to become more effective learners. That is to say we want them to become learners who are autonomous; capable of finding the information they need; sensitive to their own preferred ways of learning; and confident to attempt problems of a type they have previously not met.

Effective teachers help their children to become more confident and independent learners by offering them a range of different learning experiences and, then, by encouraging them to reflect upon these (Ainscow and Muncey, 1989).

Another feature that seems to be common to the work of many effective teachers is an emphasis on giving pupils choice (Wang and Peverley, 1987). This can have a number of positive effects.

First of all, allowing children to choose, to some extent, what they do, how and when, is a way of encouraging understanding. It allows children some opportunity to relate classroom activities to their own experiences and their existing knowledge. Indeed I would go so far as to say that as teachers we must find ways of ensuring that children bring aspects of their personal culture into the classroom in order to facilitate meaning but, also, as a source of enrichment. Too often, for example, children from other countries or families that have adopted unusual life styles are seen as 'having problems'. Instead we need to recognise that they bring with them knowledge, ideas and perspectives that can be used to illuminate the understanding of those with whom they come into contact.

Secondly, encouraging pupils to choose can help teachers to get better at setting tasks and activities more appropriately. Children know things about themselves that we can never know. Consequently we can utilise their self-knowledge by inviting them to participate in classroom decision-making (Ainscow and Tweddle, 1988).

Thirdly, choice is a way of helping children to take more responsibility for their own learning. Simply by offering it, the teacher is suggesting to the class that their views are important and that they are trusted to make significant decisions. Giving children trust and respect encourages them to value themselves as learners.

Children need help as well as encouragement to choose. First of all, of course, there have to be things to choose from; hence the need for variety of experience. Secondly, they need explanations and examples of how to make choices.

Reflection and review

I have already emphasised the importance of knowing about pupils, their skills and knowledge, their interests and attitudes, and their previous experiences. Teachers learn more about the members of their classes by careful observation and systematic monitoring of their progress (Ainscow, 1988a; Ysseldyke and Christenson, 1987). Clearly this is another of the noticeable skills of successful teachers (Rosenshine, 1983). Through their methods of monitoring they evaluate the decisions they have made in terms of their appropriateness for individual members of the class. They also give children comments on the way they are attempting to carry out their tasks.

It is important to recognise the importance of this form of feedback. Children learn as a result of their successes *and* their failures. Consequently, feedback from their teacher, or their classmates, can provide guidance and encouragement that will help them to improve their performance. In particular their errors should be corrected as soon as possible to prevent these from being practised (Engelmann, 1977). A child's efforts can usually be characterised in one of the following ways:

- incorrect and lacking understanding
- incorrect but careless
- correct but hesitant
- correct, quick and firm

Understanding which of these it is helps in deciding what action is necessary. Some activities lend themselves to children taking responsibility for monitoring their own progress, possibly by keeping some form of written record (Ainscow and Muncey, 1989).

One very useful approach is at the end of an activity, or, indeed, at the end of the day, to get children to talk in pairs or small groups about what they have been doing, what they have achieved, what is its significance and how they feel about it. My experience is that if children (even quite young children) are given guidance and encouragement they will become very actively involved in this form of self-review, often surprising their teachers by their understanding and sensitivity.

Flexible use of resources

Teaching is essentially about the use of time, the pupils' time and the teachers's time (Anderson, 1984). Well organised classrooms are geared to facilitate the effective use of time. Materials and equipment are stored in a way that enables them to be located when needed, thus allowing children to be relatively independent of the teacher.

On the other hand in less well-organised classrooms pupils remain dependent on their teacher for materials, corrections, and decisions about the direction of their work. Consequently the teacher's time is drained away dealing with routine organisational and administrative matters.

The two most significant resources for learning in any classroom are the teacher and the pupils. The use of their time is, therefore, critical to effective teaching and learning.

It is often when children are asked to carry out activities independently that most difficulties occur (Rosenshine, 1983). The teacher faces the difficulty of how to ensure that all members of the class are working appropriately; the children face possible difficulties as they work with less direction and supervision.

The aim of independent activity is often to enable pupils to practise and apply previously acquired skills and knowledge. Opportunities for extended practice can, under certain circumstances, be significant in helping children to succeed where they had previously failed (Ainscow and Tweddle, 1979). They are of little benefit, however, if a child has not got the skills and understanding necessary for completing the given task with a reasonable level of success. Hence the art is to know when children have reached a stage in their learning at which they can be left to carry on with less supervision.

Often when pupils experience difficulties with their work it is as a result of their setting off without a firm understanding of what they are doing (Bennett, *et al.*, 1984; Hull, 1985; Rosenshine, 1983). In other words their lack of success is, at least in part, an outcome of the teacher's inadequacies in introducing new ideas or material, and in providing effective forms of guided practice. It further emphasises the need for careful monitoring of children's understanding during the early stages of learning about new ideas or when developing new skills.

The teacher's movement during periods of independent activity can also be an important factor in keeping pupils involved in their assigned tasks (Rosenshine and Berliner, 1978). Effective teachers tend to be very active, encouraging and praising the children's efforts. They try to keep these interactions short and to the point in order that attention is shared around all members of the class. Invariably where a teacher finds that she is having to spend long periods re-explaining points to a lot of individuals this is an indication that the initial explanations and periods of guided practice were in some way inadequate.

The implication of all of this is that the teacher needs to manage time in ways that allow maximum opportunity for interaction with children, as a whole class, in groups and individually, that are focused on important aspects of the learning activities that are taking place. This is surely the most important priority.

Co-operative learning

An important way in which teachers can find time for all of this is to be more effective in their use of the other major resource for learning in any classroom – the pupils.

The ideas presented in this chapter assume that classrooms are places where children and adults are skilful in working together, sharing their ideas and supporting one another. They are based on the assumption that there are, as I have suggested, two major resources for learning, the teacher and the children. They also assume that teachers have skills in organising their classes in ways that encourage co-operation.

on group problem-solving within the curriculum, it is not uncommon to see pupils working alone for large parts of the school day (Galton and Simon, 1980). Often they are seated in groups, but it is still quite rare to see them carrying out their tasks collaboratively. It is difficult to know why this is so, although one possible explanation is that many teachers have not received training in ways of organising group work in the classroom.

Whilst working alone on individualised tasks is an important and legitimate approach for all children, used excessively it is a limited and limiting form of learning. This has been recognised in many schools, where attempts are being made to encourage pupils to become more skilful in learning co-operatively. This is not an easy task since it requires a sophistication of curriculum planning and implementation for which many teachers feel ill-prepared. It also requires materials that encourage children to collaborate (Lunzer et al., 1984).

Where pupils are to be introduced to co-operative ways of working this has to be planned and introduced in a systematic way, as with any other new learning experience. Effectively it involves the introduction of an additional series of demands, requiring pupils to work towards objectives associated with the content of the curriculum at the same time as achieving new objectives to do with their skills in collaboration.

When this works well, the benefits are enormous. Co-operative learning that is successful can have a positive effect on academic outcomes, self-esteem, social relationships and personal development (Johnson and Johnson, 1986). Furthermore it has the potential to free teacher time as a result of making pupils less dependent on the teacher for help and support.

It is important to recognise that co-operative learning assumes a planned approach that goes well beyond a simple commitment to encouraging children to work together (Slavin, 1988). It requires, for example, careful attention to:

(1) The setting of tasks in ways that necessitate collaboration.
(2) Helping children to recognise that their success is dependent to some degree upon the success of the other members of their group.
(3) Group size and membership that are appropriate, given the skills and experience of the children, and the nature of the tasks that are set.
(4) The development of the pupils' skills in aspects of group working, including communication, sharing and decision making.

I should add that where I have seen teachers being successful in increasing their use of co-operative learning approaches, this often seems to have been in the context of a whole school development. In other words, co-operative learning in the classroom is facilitated by co-operative planning in the staffroom.

Staff development

The suggestions I have made in this chapter are intended to be used by teachers as a basis for reviewing their own practice with a view to pin-pointing areas for development. My assumption is that as teachers we should all continue to see ourselves as learners, seeking to improve our work in the light of a continual process of reflecting upon experience.

The area of staff development is central to this process of professional reflection and development. Indeed I would argue that where schools are seeking to move towards a whole school approach for dealing with special needs, successful staff development is essential. Evidence from extensive research on staff development in education (e.g. Ainscow and Muncey, 1989; Joyce and Showers, 1988; Powers, 1983) indicates the importance of the following elements:

● Understanding of theory and purpose
An exploration of theory through discussion, lectures or reading is necessary for an understanding of the rationale behind new teaching procedures. Teachers need to understand what they are to do and why.

● Demonstration

The modelling of new teaching approaches facilitates their introduction. They may be presented on video, observed on a visit to
another school or, ideally, conducted live in the teacher's own
classroom.

● Practice and feedback

In order to become confident in the use of a new teaching
approach teachers need opportunity to practise and receive constructive feedback as they practise. Again ideally this should
occur in the teacher's usual classroom. An obvious way for this
to occur is to make timetable arrangements for colleagues to
spend periods working together. This idea, sometimes called
'peer coaching', has been shown to be very effective in encouraging the implementation of new ways of teaching. It provides
support as a group of colleagues attempt to master new skills;
technical feedback on the congruence of practice trials with ideal
performance; and companionships and collegial problem solving
as new skills are integrated with existing behaviours and
implemented in the classroom.

As schools attempt to develop their policies for meeting special needs,
therefore, they need to devise a co-ordinated plan for staff development that allows teachers to support one another as they seek to
improve their practice. In so doing the emphasis must be on building
upon the existing knowledge and expertise within the school. The
suggestions in this chapter are offered as my contribution to this
process.

References

Ainscow, M. (1988) 'Beyond the eyes of the monster: An analysis of recent
trends in assessment and recording'. *Support for Learning*, 3(3): 149–153.

Ainscow, M. and Muncey, J. (1989) *Meeting Individual Needs in the Primary
School*. London: Fulton.

Ainscow, M. and Tweddle, D. A. (1979) *Preventing Classroom Failure*.
Chichester: Wiley.

Ainscow, M. and Tweddle, D. A. (1988) *Encouraging Classroom Success*.
London: Fulton.

Anderson, L. W. (ed.) (1984) *Time and School Learning*. London: Croom
Helm.

Bennett, N., Desforges, C., Cockburn, A. and Wilkinson, B. (1984) *The
Quality of Pupil Learning Experiences* London: Erlbaum.

Brophy, J. E. (1983) 'Classroom organisation and management'. *The Elementary School Journal*, 82: 266–285.

Engelmann, S. E. (1977) 'Sequencing cognitive and academic tasks'. In Kneedler R. D. and Tarver S. G. (eds.) *Changing Perspectives in Special Education*. Columbus: Merrill.

Galton, M. J. and Simon, B. (1980) *Progress and Performance in the Primary Classroom*. London: RKP.

Hull, R. (1985) *The Language Gap*. London: Methuen.

Johnson, D. W. and Johnson, R. T. (1986) 'Mainstreaming and co-operative learning strategies'. *Exceptional Children*, 52: 553–561.

Joyce, B. and Showers, B. (1988) *Student Achievement Through Staff Development*. London: Longman.

Kounin, J. (1970) *Discipline and Group Management in Classrooms*. New York: Holt, Rinehart and Winston.

Lunzer, E., Gardner, K., Davies, F. and Green, T. (1984) *Learning from the Written Word*. Edinburgh: Oliver and Boyd.

Mortimore, P., Sammons, P., Stoll, L., Lewis, D. and Ecob, R. (1988) *School Matters: The Junior Years*. Exeter: Open Books.

Porter, A. C. and Brophy, J. (1988) 'Synthesis of research on good teaching'. *Educational Leadership*, **48** (8): 74–85.

Powers, D. A. (1983) 'Mainstreaming and the inservice education of teachers'. *Exceptional Children*, **49**: 432–439.

Rosenshine, B. (1983) 'Teacher functions in instructional programmes'. *The Elementary School Journal*, **83**: 335–351.

Rosenshine, B. and Berliner, D. C. (1978) 'Academic engaged time'. *British Journal of Teacher Education*, 4: 3–16.

Slavin, R. E. (1988) 'Cooperative Learning and Student Achievement'. *Educational Leadership* **6**: 31–33.

Walberg, H. J. and Wang, M. C. (1987) 'Effective educational practices and provision for individual differences'. In Wang, M. C., Reynolds M. C., and Walberg, H. J., (eds.) *Handbook of Special Education: Research and Practice Volume 1*. Oxford: Pergamon.

Wang, M. C. and Peverley, S. T. (1987) 'The role of the learner: An individual difference variable in school learning and functioning'. In Wang, M. C., Reynolds, M. C., and Walberg, H. J., (eds) *Handbook of Special Education: Research and Practice Volume 1*. Oxford: Pergamon.

Wells, G. (1986) *The Meaning Makers: Children Using Language and Using Language to Learn*. London: Hodder and Stoughton.

Ysseldyke, J. E. and Christenson, S. L. (1987) 'Evaluating students' instructional environments'. *Remedial and Special Education*, **8** (3): 17–24.

CHAPTER 10

On Being a Support Teacher

Lois Hockley

'The support teacher for the management of 10–14 year old children with emotional/behaviour difficulties' is a post created as one of Banbury's responses to the Warnock Report. After the publication of the report in 1978 the Banbury area began to make new responses to a wide range of special educational needs through changes in the ordinary schools.

The Banbury area of the Oxfordshire Education Authority is divided into sectors, each comprising a comprehensive school and its associated primary schools. Different approaches are being tried out in different sectors including the creation of the post I held from 1981 to December 1984.

Definition of the support teacher's role

As support teacher for children with emotional and behaviour difficulties, I have been working in two comprehensive schools and 10 feeder primary schools. Within all these schools my short-term emphasis has been on individual pupils and on help to staff in the most advantageous methods of managing children. My long-term emphasis, where appropriate, has been on extending the skills and expertise of class teachers. I am *not* a resource room teacher offering regular part-time tuition; or a crisis teacher responding to crises; or a 'time out' teacher supervising the removal of pupils from the ordinary classroom.

I have perceived my role as including three major functions:

classroom work and visits; liaison and coordination; and in-service training.

Classroom work and visits

From the start the work has been primarily in the classroom. My aim has been to support the teacher or child as necessary, not to undermine the authority of the teacher and his or her responsibility for the pupils during lessons. Children with special educational needs in the ordinary school should not be made conspicuous through being the only ones to receive extra attention, so support has been given generally during the lessons. If the class teacher has been teaching the entire class I have been able to help in managing children causing disruption or needing extra encouragement. When children have been working independently the teacher has helped the 'special needs' pupils while I have given general support to the remainder of the class.

The work in the classroom entails the elements described below.

● Flexibility
  This is essential because of the highly individual balance between a child's capacity to adjust and what the environment expects, provides and enforces. A blanket approach to children is therefore impossible.

● Observation
  A pupil's attitude to self, peers, adults, physical and other environmental conditions needs to be observed.

● Problem classification and suggestions for different approach
  These are governed by schools' circumstances, current pressures on teachers and the personalities of the staff. The support teacher needs to decide whether it is possible to add to the staff's management techniques, to suggest acceptable ways of changing the child's behaviour, or to consider transferring the child to another setting.

● Monitoring
  This is necessary in order: to assess the child's progress and to report any improvements to the teacher who, because of close daily contact with the child, may not have been fully aware of them; to support pupils who spend a session at the tutorial unit or who have left another hall or school; to observe changes in a child's behaviour across settings.

● Consultations with staff
These are more general in nature and the purpose is to reinforce and encourage individual class teachers and staff or departments who are teaching or about to teach a problematic pupil or class.

Besides work in the 10 primary schools, I have also visited classes in the two comprehensive schools in order to follow up individual children who have transferred to them from the primary schools, or to respond to requests from the teachers for me to join their lessons and give support to individual children or a whole class. My work in the comprehensive schools has appeared more 'passive' – never being in control of the situation, but backing up the teacher's work. It has not really been passive, however. Presenting ideas on how to manage pupils within the constraints of a conventional lesson is a constantly demanding task.

Liaison and coordination

Being in a primary school throughout the year, I have been asked to provide information (gathered from the primary school staff and personal observation) which may help in placing a child within a comprehensive school and easing subsequent transfer. This has benefited not only the obviously damaged child but it has helped many more children with mild learning difficulties, social or other disadvantages (Wall, 1979; DES, 1978).

Within one comprehensive school, I have visited each new intake class during its two pre-entry visits, and again on the first day of term to help, if necessary, any upset children. I have joined the first year classes near the beginning of the year when their tutor is teaching them in case further discussions are beneficial, and have reviewed the first year children with the year heads in each hall after half a term and at the end of the year. Discussions with the heads of the second year have occurred at the beginning and end of the academic year.

When the children have transferred from one hall or school to another because of difficulties, it has been necessary to consider: placement within a new group, the tutor, possible welfare assistance, possible continuing support from an off-site unit, and how support can be given to the child, teacher and parents.

Some pupils need extra help at secondary level in order to gain self respect and self confidence. This has been made possible by the marvellous cooperation of the staff of the hostel for primary children during the school week. They have allowed a girl to help with domestic work one morning weekly, and teenagers to organise discos for the hostel children. Another girl benefited from helping in a primary school with the younger children.

Regular group discussions with the staff teaching the child have been an aim. These take place informally and incidentally in the staffroom without the support teacher's presence and may not include all staff teaching the pupil. On other occasions I have asked staff teaching a class to come together either to discuss a child or to consider the class in which the child has lessons, which may be a difficult group.

There have been discussions with parents whose children suffer from behaviour or learning difficulties or from transfer anxieties, or who are reluctant to accept remedial education for their child. Fortnightly discussions with parents, the social worker and tutors have provided very supportive relationships for all concerned, likewise work with family and child guidance personnel and other relevant agencies.

I have attended case conferences mainly in comprehensive schools and often, unfortunately, when a crisis has already been reached. Who should attend, who are most familiar with the child within the school, who is going to carry out agreed recommendations, and whether or not parents should be involved all need to be considered. I have found that parents are not brought into school at an early enough stage.

In-service training

The children have generally been fully integrated in the primary school and this continues within the comprehensive schools. Whether or not a child is considered handicapped and consequently in need of more specialised help depends on his or her ability to meet the expectations of the ordinary school. This in turn depends on what the school offers and expects. If the curriculum is made appropriate many problems cease to exist.

Consequently 'in service' help needs to be given to individuals, groups or entire staff. I have also, on request, led staff discussions on curriculum areas and workshops on management of behaviour difficulties. Some staff have asked for help with readability of work sheets so that behaviour difficulties do not occur through inappropriate work.

I have joined discussions and working parties on records, reports, organisation and curriculum and, to assist staff in the sectors, I have started a reference library including books, tests and catalogues. I have also had meetings with welfare assistants who, until summer 1982, had little experience of working in comprehensive, mainstream classes, just as the teaching staff had not experienced this type of assistance before, with another person in their classrooms.

The curriculum and in-service training have been very important to me. There is much talk about the needs of children, much less about the needs of staff who feel threatened by the prospect of integration and require support.

Assessments and requirements of the role

To bridge the primary-secondary divide, develop strategies for teachers and ancillaries in the ordinary classroom, and to avoid or solve management problems (Sayer, 1983) I have had to get to know the schools, their physical layout and staff resources, so as to be able to suggest alternative management strategies.

As support teacher I have always tried to keep in mind the needs and perspectives of others as well as my own.

If I were the teacher or head, for instance, I might ask the following questions. What would my reaction be to a second person in the room? Would I like to go somewhere outside the school to discuss problems and use reference books? Do I need to wait until there is a large problem before discussing it? If I had a problem with a child, to whom could I turn in order to share it? How much parent contact would I like to have to get the complete picture? Do I have the time?

If I were the child I might ask two questions. Do I know who is in control of the class on this or other occasions? Do I use all the adults in the room to get all the assistance possible with my work?

As support teacher I have asked myself the following questions. What would I do if I were the class teacher in a particular situation? How is the teacher going to react to what I do or say? Is the time right for a major issue to be discussed? Have I considered the role constraints and the risks of intruding upon another professional's domain? Is the involvement of yet another person with the child, family or teacher desirable? (So many personnel, particularly in comprehensive schools, could be involved with the particular child.) Is there any degree of conflicting advice? Am I aware of the appropriate resources within the immediate area or county that might assist with this problem?

Although my role has been described as walking a continuous tightrope, it is a fascinating one with one special advantage. Not being attached to a particular school permits greater objectivity. An office in a 'neutral zone' is also helpful.

Reactions of others to the role

Cooperation within the primary schools has been marvellous with mutual support and shared understanding in the management of behaviour problems. Primary teachers have enjoyed the feedback I have given them on their former pupils who have gone on to secondary schools. There is a continuum of interest and openness of discussion between staff across age groups.

However, the introduction of my particular support role within the comprehensive school has proved uncomfortable and personally threatening to a minority of staff, some of whom have actually resisted it.

I appreciate that any second adult in the classroom can affect the teacher's rapport with the class and the behaviour of a child or class, especially if the classroom has traditionally been one adult's domain – the reason usually given for resistance. I do, however, ask myself if the class teacher has considered how a support teacher can contribute.

Although there is a danger of diverting pupils' attention away from the class teacher and creating a slight change of atmosphere, a support teacher's presence can enable the teacher and class to have a better 'run' at a subject without disruption.

I have also had to consider the other half-voiced concerns – fully understood by anyone who has worked in a comprehensive school – that, for instance, there has not been time to do adequate preparation for a group, that examination pressures for one group diminish preparation time for another, that personal commitments may take priority, that there is no knowing what will be said to whom about a lesson. From the start, however, I have resisted being drawn into discussions about various professionals and schools. I strongly believe in loyalty to each school and each individual in it.

The nature of pupils' problem behaviour can determine the reaction of some secondary school staff to the support teacher. While appreciating the feelings aroused by disruptive acts I have felt that some teachers' unwillingness to discuss them and their defensiveness (to offset implied personal failure and the hierarchical pastoral care system) can impair both staff and children (Galloway *et al.*, 1982; Murgatroyd, 1980; Tattum, 1982). Early discussion of problems with the support teacher could lead to earlier easing of the situation, retaining of the teacher's respect and morale, and prevention, rather than the crisis measures which are needed when a problem has escalated into a major confrontation.

Conclusion

My teaching experience in primary, middle and secondary schools, and as a peripatetic teacher in a reading advisory service centre, has enabled me to appreciate the different pressures on staff and the support that some teachers are willing to accept.

My work within the primary schools has been most enjoyable and it has been a pleasure to join with those secondary teachers who have asked for my support. Feedback from comprehensive school staff has varied. I have appreciated the response of staff who have reported improvements and successes and have even invited me to join a lesson to see for myself.

The information gained during a child's last year in junior school and shared with comprehensive school colleagues has been valuable and has helped to prevent problems from arising or recurring. To be associated with individuals and groups of children who have gained self confidence and self respect from activities both within and outside the school is stimulating and challenging.

The quality of work with teachers and other professionals has depended on: the quality of, and response to, the information flow; confidentiality and trust; the quality of contacts, free from 'pulling rank'; the professional's advice reflecting his own concerns, leaving others to concentrate on their own expertise (Galloway et al., 1982).

A support teacher can influence the organisation of the ordinary school by gradually feeding in ideas. However, changing attitudes and roles within comprehensive schools increase anxieties, which must be taken into account.

This support role is vital in helping staff to share and develop professional knowledge, although for some staff more threatening and emotive than the role of the support teacher for a specific subject. If instead pupils attend support centres or special classes they are prevented from pursuing a wide range of subjects and examinations, and their reintegration into class or school may be hindered. Off-site provision may also be seen by some teachers as an opportunity to avoid facing up to the problems created by the ethos of the schools (Mortimore et al., 1983).

As Nicholls (1983) has written: 'In the promotion of educational innovation, which is so influenced by its own particular setting and by the participants, no guarantees of success or even do-it-yourself manuals can be offered'.

This is only an outline of the role. The author would willingly

88

discuss more specific examples with individuals about to undertake such a role or already working in a similar manner.

[This article was first published in *British Journal of Special Education* Vol. 12, No. 1: March 1985.]

References

Department of Education and Science (1978) *Special Educational Needs* (Warnock Report). London: HMSO.

Galloway, D., Ball, T., Bloomfield, D., and Seyd, R. (1982) *Schools and Disruptive Pupils*. London: Longman.

Jones, N. J. (1983) 'The Management of Integration'. In Booth, T. and Potts, P. *Integrating Special Education*. Oxford: Blackwell.

Mortimore, P., Davies, J., Varlaam, A., and West, A. (1983) *Behaviour Problems in Schools. An evaluation of support centres*. London: Croom Helm.

Murgatroyd, S. (ed.) (1980) *Helping the Troubled Child*. London: Harper and Row.

Nicholls, A. (1983) *Managing Educational Innovations*. London: George Allen and Unwin.

Sayer, J. (1983) 'Assessment for all, statements for none?' *Special Education: Forward Trends*, **10**, (4): 15–16.

Tattum, D. P. (1982) *Disruptive Pupils in Schools and Units*. London: Croom Helm.

Wall, W. D. (1979) *Constructive Education for Special Groups*. London: Harrap.

CHAPTER 11

Support Teaching: Taking a Closer Look

Jean Garnett

Schools tend to set up initiatives to support children with special educational needs within the ordinary classroom before they have fully considered the issues, implications, and conditions crucial to success. Are they aware, for instance, that unless the headteacher and senior management are seen as taking a decisive lead, the chances of strong initial support for change are limited? Do they appreciate that the majority of the school staff must have the will the make the new system work if it is to get off to a good start? Do they realise that the professional and personal relationships between support teacher and subject teacher are crucial to the effectiveness of a support system?

The aim of this chapter is to encourage successful practice by

(1) examining what is meant by 'classroom support'
(2) identifying some of the issues, questions and problems
(3) giving examples of current practice and observations made by teachers taking part
(4) presenting some of the factors now recognised as influencing the development of effective classroom support
(5) offering a possible framework for the role of the support teacher.

As Bines (1986) implies, changing to the practice of supporting mainstream teachers within the classroom means that a school is redefining the role of its remedial/special education teachers from working separately with a special or withdrawal group to working in partnership. That children with learning difficulties can learn from a mainstream curriculum, and that the 'support teacher' model is better than the more traditional ones are probably the most important assumptions on which this approach is based. But the main conviction must be that special educational needs are the responsibility of the whole staff and not merely a specially appointed few.

Defining classroom support

The traditional role of remedial teachers was mainly seen as assessing, diagnosing and teaching clearly identified children, usually on a temporary withdrawal basis, or in a special class. The new partnership role is broader, boundaries are less clear, and a new set of skills is needed. The task might include offering advice and help, sharing ideas and expertise, developing strategies for assessment and monitoring of progress within the context of the school's curriculum, evaluating the curriculum, and promoting cooperation with other agencies.

Classroom support can be seen as having three main aspects, as described below.

In-class support A second teacher works alongside the subject teacher for some lessons. This teacher may be one of the school's special needs support (remedial) teachers, a colleague from the subject teacher's own department or any other colleague who has an extra non-teaching period available.

Curriculum development support Strategies and appropriate materials are developed to help *all* the pupils in the class to understand and respond positively to the lesson content.

Tutorial support Tutorial help is provided to meet specific learning needs as they emerge. This may be offered in class or arranged in a special needs resource room

Some issues, questions and problems posed by teachers

Trying to translate the three aspects into practice brings certain questions to mind.

☐ Which staff give classroom support – only the special educators or are other teachers included?

☐ What *are* the different responsibilities of the support teacher and the subject teacher and where do their roles converge?

☐ Which of the two is responsible for making the lesson coherent and accessible for the pupils with learning difficulties or do they share the responsibility?

☐ How are the individual needs of the pupils met in these circumstances?

These are just some of the questions aired by teacher colleagues during in-service sessions in which they had discussed how to make support teaching work. They illustrate the complexity of the issues which emerge as people set about the task.

Support teachers need to develop particular skills in working with colleagues if special educational needs are to be met effectively within the mainstream class, and if subject teachers are to acquire the confidence and expertise to cope with the responsibilities. These skills will include the capacity to

listen and understand colleagues' concerns

decide on priorities for action

anticipate colleagues' as well as pupils' needs and respond positively

offer a range of alternative approaches, methods, strategies and resources to meet pupils' differing needs

grasp the essentials of most subject areas and so assist in curriculum development and planning

be constructive and encouraging rather than threatening to colleagues' self or professional esteem, but know when to stand firm

know whom to refer to for further advice both within and outside school

be flexible in negotiating who should do what in the classroom.

In-service training for the support teachers with, and *alongside*, their mainstream colleagues is therefore a major requirement for truly positive outcomes.

Current practice and observations

An example of in-class support

A support teacher in a large, inner city comprehensive school with a high proportion of Asian and West Indian children, saw her work as a classroom support teacher in terms of benefits, problems and concerns (Figure 11.1). She was timetabled to offer support to English teachers

Figure 11.1 The verbatim observations of a support teacher

Benefits	Problems	Concerns
1 I can help more pupils.	Supporting only one lesson can result in lack of continuity	Meeting the needs of all pupils requiring help is difficult
2 Pupils also seem more willing to seek help	Absence of one teacher may not be covered	'Watering down' of basic skill learning can happen
3 Learning problems are dealt with as they rise	Lateness of either teacher causes problems for the other	Time is needed for both teachers to evaluate and prepare lessons
4 All support teaching can relate to the classwork	Some subject teachers want to 'offload' their most difficult pupils onto the support teacher	Some extra-tutorial help is needed for some pupils
5 Ideas, resources approaches can be shared		Some lessons are not appropriate for support teaching
		Implications arise for joint planning of lessons

for one lesson a week in each of the first year classes. She was not only expected to look to the needs of identified children but to support any pupils who found themselves in difficulties, as they emerged. Her role as support teacher was not always clearly agreed with her colleague and she was asking for guidance on how to solve this difficulty tactfully. She found that her effectiveness largely depended on the goodwill of the subject teachers. Some valued her presence and took it seriously while others were uncertain about having a second teacher in the class and felt vaguely threatened.

Comment In many schools staff willingness and availability, and timetable flexibility, largely govern the choice and number of lessons to be supported. The role that the support teacher takes in the class tends to come second on the priority list. The overt reasons for this are linked with staff shortages but there are also underlying factors to do with the kind of recognition and therefore importance laid by the school on its provision for meeting needs in general. The stress that many teachers lay on the *products* of their teaching rather than the *processes* of learning also influences the role the support teacher plays.

A contrasting example

A support teacher in a large suburban comprehensive described her experiences in two different English classes. Here again she was able to cover only one lesson a week for each class. The two subject teachers saw the support teacher's contribution differently. Figure 11.2 illustrates how those differing views affected the personal and professional relationship between the two teachers and the influence this had on the support teacher's effectiveness.

This experience demonstrated clearly to her how necessary it is for the classteacher's views to be considered before an innovation of this kind is put into practice. Teacher B was obviously not ready to take on board another teacher and did not understand the purpose or how it might ease her task. She may also have been conscious of weakness in her own lesson planning and teaching which a regular visitor would – and did – detect. She felt pressurised and vulnerable, a state which would not necessarily be mitigated however friendly and tactful the support teacher might be. For her part the support teacher felt uncomfortable, undermined and devalued.

Comment Where the principle of classroom support has been accepted by all the teachers in a school or department the will to make it work does seem to develop. In spite of all the problems people set about re-thinking their approaches and finding ways to overcome difficulties. The Tile Hill Wood model is an example of this (Giles and Dunlop, 1986).

Observations

Observations made by teachers from various schools illustrate the quality, depth and breadth of thinking which can go into finding ways to make classroom support work.

> Another possibility would be for the four mainstream teachers and their support teacher to work as a team, drawing up a detailed support programme which would then be operated by the support teacher. Pupils for whom extra and relevant tuition was needed could be withdrawn for short periods at pre-arranged times. (Maths teacher)
>
> Ideally, in my opinion, a support teacher should be attached for a reasonable length of time to one particular host teacher. I would

Figure 11.2 Differing attitudes of subject teachers

ORGANISATION

OUTCOMES

Teacher A: autumn term

1 Cooperative teaching with lead lesson prepared by either class teacher (CT) or support teacher (ST)

2 Both were informed beforehand on what was to be done

3 Follow-up work (e.g. marking, tutorial) carried out by both

4 ST did not necessarily focus on specified pupils

1 Lessons were well planned and organised by shared expertise

2 Both teachers understood what was going on

3 Regular contact and discussion built up professional relationship

4 Workload was shared so preparation was simpler

5 CT and ST saw each other as equally necessary and valued

6 A positive learning atmosphere developed

7 Professional confidence and trust grew

Spring term

1 Both teachers agreed on a blitz on reading: fluency for the whole class

2 SRA Reading Lab. introduced and explained

3 Both helped individual pupils

Summer term

1 As for first half of autumn term

2 Second half, small groups for reading activities

3 Both teachers circulated all groups

Result

1 An integrated, purposefully learning class

Teacher B: autumn term

1 ST 'allowed' into lesson

2 No previous sharing of lesson content; CT actively discouraged this

3 ST spend much time trying to discover content of lesson

4 Lessons unstructured

1 Little cooperation or sharing of planning or expertise

2 CT's attitude made ST feel inferior

3 No relationship developed between them

4 Therefore little trust or confidence built

5 ST discouraged and uninvolved

Spring and summer terms

1 ST decided to withdraw a small group for literacy and confidence building

2 CT continued as before

Result

1 Support teacher eventually withdrew the group. 'I felt as if I was at least doing something positive'.

advocate a minimum of half a term. Within the relationship between the teachers, there must be the flexibility to adapt the model so that small numbers (even individuals) can be withdrawn for more intensive assistance.

'Support teaching' is a concept and practice to be encouraged because my experience, although far from satisfactory, has shown that when operated well, and with teachers who have respect for each other, the children gain appreciably. (Special needs teacher)

Some needs identified by an English teacher were:

A clear definition of the roles of mainstream and support teachers. Understanding about where responsibilities lie; for instance, for discipline, marking and setting of homework.

The support teacher needs to know *what* the mainstream teacher is going to teach and *when* – a framework of events.

Above all we need time. Relying on good rapport between teachers is not enough. For all to make the best use of their skills regular meetings are needed to discuss approaches and evaluate lessons.

Influencing factors

Factors which have an important influence on the development of effective classroom support were identified by the teachers making the observations quoted above. These include:

- the level of consensus across the whole school staff on adopting such a system and their awareness of the implications it raises for the school as a whole
- the importance of pre-planning and sharing of curriculum content between the participating teachers before it starts
- making sure that the subject teacher is clear about what to expect of the support teacher (confused perceptions of the role hamper progress)
- availability of time for tutorial provision and preparation of learning resources; classroom support is expensive on time, freeing the appropriate staff for such work is difficult and providing cover for teachers to meet during the school day (other than at coffee or lunch break) costs money and affects continuity
- the kind of working relationship struck up by the two teachers and the confidence and value they place on each other's capacity to contribute equally

● the ability of each to recognise the other's strengths and defer to the other without feeling inferior or undermined.

It was a short step for these teachers from identifying the factors to setting questions to consider as they embarked on the practice.

☐ What can the two teachers *do* to establish a harmonious working relationship before they start working together in the classroom?

☐ How can the two teachers find the time to liaise?

☐ How often do they need to meet outside the classroom?

☐ In what ways can the support teacher help with planning and preparation?

☐ What resources do they need and which of them is going to prepare what?

☐ Should they work out a joint record system?

☐ How will they evaluate the effectiveness of their joint work?

☐ How should classroom order and discipline be managed when the support teacher is present?

The question of who has responsibility for discipline evokes some concerns especially for those support and subject teachers who have difficulties keeping order in the classroom. It is a matter which needs sensitive handling but the ultimate responsibility must lie with the regular teacher of the class, whatever is agreed on occasions between the two teachers. How responsibility is worked out will depend on many variables but chiefly on the relationships which exist within the triangle of subject teacher, support teacher and pupils. Little is gained and much is lost if the subject teacher lets go of this vital responsibility and effective support must aim to strengthen that teacher's capacity to retain it.

Members of the group which formulated these questions went back to their schools intending to find solutions. They hoped to reconvene in a few months to consider and evaluate some of the steps they had taken.

The role of the support teacher – a framework

It is ironic that as one explores more deeply into the many aspects of support teaching and their implications the notion of 'support' begins to get in the way.

Ultimately what we are talking about is the practice of two colleagues with certain expertise and responsibilities who can work together in the classroom to enhance the learning of pupils in a particular class. Two in harmonious collaboration add up to more than the sum of one and one.

This notion gives rise to a further cautionary thought. In such circumstances could the role of the support teacher become so loosely defined as to make the schools' special needs provision more vulnerable to staff cuts than it is already? Could the result be that the needs of too many children would not be met precisely enough? For this reason classroom support, however practised, must be three-fold in concept. That third element, as stated in the section on 'Defining classroom support', is tutorial support geared to meet precise needs and flexible enough to provide a variety of responses. Such provision is expensive and calls for a commitment by the LEA as well as school management to the approach. Perhaps such is the ideal.

Meanwhile we can but start at the 'coping' point. With this in mind suggestions for the role of the support teacher are offered here as a framework for discussion and negotiation. The list (Figure 11.3) must not be seen as a definitive statement but rather as the 'starter for 10'.

Figure 11.3 Role of the support teacher – a framework for discussion

The following responsibilities are suggested as appropriate to the support teacher

1 To work in collaboration with the class/subject teacher to make the curriculum accessible/understandable for all pupils in the class and to help with planning of the supported lesson.

2 To assist in identifying individual pupils' needs in order to help them over their learning obstacles and set appropriate objectives.

3 To help to provide effective learning strategies which can be incorporated into the work of particular pupils.

4 To assist in developing resource materials to meet individual needs.

5 To develop a variety of methods which individual pupils may be offered to enhance their learning (finding pathways to learning).

6 To assist in providing methods for marking, assessment and recording which can be practised by both teachers.

7 To assist in the continual evaluation of the approaches, methods and materials being offered to all the class and especially for the pupils with special learning needs.

8 To help find ways to provide individual tuition when needed.

Giving tutorial support

By 'tutorial help' is meant a regular allotted time when pupils may go for specific help to overcome a particular learning obstacle. The tutorial may be for an individual or group and is different from the traditional remedial withdrawal system in two ways. Firstly it is specific to and in context with the child's classwork; secondly it deals with individuals' difficulties as they arise.

It should be organised – and be seen – to be available to any pupil requiring it, the aim being to develop the notion that every pupil has individual learning problems. This kind of practice should underline the fact that equality of treatment is recognising that all children are different.

Conclusion

The principles underlying the practice of classroom support demand greater changes within a school than may be realised at first. They look to the breakdown of all sorts of embedded assumptions and barriers.

Perhaps the most important principle to grasp is that all pupils have right of access to their school's curriculum and therefore all teachers have responsibility for identifying and responding to the special needs which emerge in their classes.

To accommodate this principle teachers are having to examine their attitudes to the boundaries of responsibility, to their notions regarding ability and intelligence and to grouping and banding of pupils and so on.

Classroom support also has profound implications for the very nature of the curriculum: how it is to be organised and delivered, and the variety of teaching skills which teachers now need to have in their repertoire. The special educators' role is most profoundly affected for these teachers are not only breaking out of what has recently been seen as a 'remedial' subject community (Bines, *op.cit.*) but breaking into other subject communities. This process demands a breadth of expertise in developing relationships not required in the past.

Here lie the professional, personal and emotional factors on which the practice of classroom support may stand or fall. What is interesting and heart warming is that when those who are involved are truly committed to it and are meeting each problem and obstacle with confidence and cooperation all the teachers seem to gain in professional strength and expertise. It still remains to be seen whether they can prove conclusively that what they are doing is better than that which has gone before in secondary schools.

[This article was first published in *British Journal of Special Education*, Volume 15, No. 1: March 1988.

Thanks are extended to all the teachers whose experiences, comments and observations contributed to the article, especially Rosemary Stokes and Sally Longdon who provided the information contained Figures 11.1 and 11.2.]

References

Bines, H. (1986) *Redefining Remedial Education*. London: Croom Helm.
Giles, C. and Dunlop, S. (1986) 'Changing direction at Tile Hill Wood'. *British Journal of Special Education* **3**, 3: 120–123. See Chapter 6.

CHAPTER 12

Which Model? Six Ways into Support

Margaret Buck

An agenda for discussion

At Tile Hill Wood School all staff are given a copy of a document about the development and current organisation of the school's support network within the school. Support guidelines are included, to serve as an agenda for discussion and decision making between the support and subject teachers (Figure 12.1).

Making decisions about support

The support teacher and the subject teacher should discuss the needs of the student(s) and if necessary consult with any other relevant professionals such as: the tutor; the head of department; the co-ordinator; the key teacher; teachers from the outside support services; the educational psychologist and so on.

With the needs of the students in mind the purposes of support should be discussed. It is possible that the subject teacher may also have needs which support can address, to the benefit of students experiences of learning. If the purposes of support are to service the needs of a department, or to resource the curriculum, discussion between all the interested parties is vital.

Generally speaking support is offered on an 'in-class' basis but supporting students outside the mainstream classroom remains an option. In-class support versus withdrawal is not an issue at Tile Hill Wood because the model of support will probably determine the appropriate context; if not, the most sensible way is to ask the student what she would prefer.

Figure 12.1 Agenda for discussion between the support and subject teacher to facilitate the support relationship

1 How can support be deployed most efficiently? What are the needs of the students? Could the curriculum be made more accessible? What difficulties can be identified? How could the support teacher best serve the needs of the students and the mainstream teacher?

2 Who will do what? With whom? Where? How? When? What advance preparation could be planned? What resources could be prepared?

3 Is it possible to pass on copies of the syllabus, the texts, the worksheets, the scheme of work, well in advance so that the support teacher can have an opportunity to become familiar with them and make a contribution to the resources that will be used?

4 How will discipline be handled? How will you deal with the normal classroom routines?

5 What arrangements can be made for economical and yet effective liaison?

6 What about the marking of students' work and assessment?

7 What records will be kept? Will they be shared or made accessible to both teachers?

8 How will the support teacher be introduced to the class to ensure that both students and teachers are comfortable with the situation?

9 What will happen if the class teacher is absent? (It is accepted that, if the class teacher is absent, he or she will be replaced by a relief teacher and the support teacher will not be expected to cover the class.)

Models for support

The support guidelines at Tile Hill Wood School offer staff a variety of models for support. Having decided on the needs of the students and how they relate to decisions concerning the support of staff and the curriculum, teachers are encouraged to choose the model which seems most appropriate to their circumstances and context of working. Support can involve:

- working with individual students
- working with a group
- facilitating collaborative or team teaching
- resourcing the curriculum
- offering small-scale INSET to the department
- tracking a student

Staff are also encouraged to try out 'new' ways of being involved in support, and then to share their experiences with others.

A The support teacher working with individual students

The aim of this model of support is to target the specific needs of individual students which should be identified before the support takes place. Support can be temporary, to meet a specific temporary need, or it can be offered long-term; where the student has more permanent needs, such as sensory impairment.

This model of support can be used to meet specific needs related to basic language and numeracy skills. Students at Tile Hill Wood may have individual help during normal lesons but also during lunchtimes, registration periods and before and after school. Programmes which are designed to be used on an individual basis can be managed through individual support sessions.

Needs arising from hearing impairment, visual impairment, speech difficulties or medical conditions can also be met in this way. For example, one student who uses a phonic aid has had individual pre- and post-lesson support for some of her GCSE courses.

Since both departments have some support time it has been possible to consider meeting students' needs across the curriculum. The key teacher for physical education has used support time to offer individual lessons to girls who have been unable to join in the normal timetabled swimming lessons. This has meant, for example, that an Asian student (who has learning difficulties and hearing impairments, as well as needs relating to English being her second language) has had the opportunity to learn to swim. She was unable to take part in previous years because she had grommets fitted. The experience has worked wonders for her self esteem. This opportunity has also been offered to students who have epilepsy.

Support offered to individuals can address needs arising from prolonged absence, illness or school transfer. For example, one girl who left the school and then returned after a term was offered extra help to enable her to cope with the demands of her modular science course.

Certain students who have needs arising from a poor self image and a lack of confidence have been offered individual curriculum support; the real intention being to boost their self esteem and to improve their confidence. Students experiencing difficulties in learning can be offered individual counselling, to develop their understanding of the processes involved and to encourage them to develop strategies to meet personal targets. Students who have limited organisational skills are encouraged and monitored in their use of planners, diaries and other strategies to 'get their act together'.

B The support teacher working with a group

Support teachers can be used to undertake small group teaching. Groups need not be grouped according to ability; there are benefits in grouping according to other criteria. In fact it is important to avoid the trap of creating 'sink groups' by continually grouping the same students according to ability.

Help can be offered to groups of students who share similar curricular needs or with certain skills. For example, this approach can be used in supporting students following the SMP mathematics course both to meet the learning needs of those who encounter difficulties and to develop the skills of those whose learning experiences need to be extended.

The small group context is less threatening to some students and it can stimulate the growth of self confidence in oral work/group discussion. It is possible for the support teacher to manage the group so that all the members have the opportunity to take part. This opportunity had been used to effect in discussions in English. Modern language oral/aural activities also lend themselves to this kind of support and first year students have gained in confidence in learning a new language.

This model of support can be used to offer a group of students the opportunity to work under closer monitoring with the purpose of developing certain skills, such as social skills. This use of support has been used to reinforce the intentions of the existing tutorial programme. Problem solving activities can also be dealt with in a more carefully monitored context; support has been deployed in practical sessions in science, craft, design, technology (CDT) and art.

There is no reason why the support teacher cannot manage the rest of the class, enabling the subject teacher to work more intensively with a small group of students. This use of support enables the subject teacher to gain knowledge about why students experience difficulties with the curriculum on offer.

C The support teacher facilitating collaborative or team teaching

Using the model of involvement in collaborative or team teaching allows for great flexibility in the use of the resource of a fellow professional. It also encourages a higher level of improvisation and spontaneity within the classroom, in response to the needs of students which may arise during the course of the lesson. But, equally, this model makes high demands in the preparation and liaison necessary for it to be effective.

It is possible to enhance the curriculum on offer by drawing on the specific subject expertise, interests, or skills of the support teacher. This encourages support teachers to get involved in subject areas other than their own; they may have personal talents and interests which are outside their subject area but which can prove useful in other areas of the curriculum.

This model enables a more experienced teacher to pass on his or her expertise to a less experienced teacher; teachers can witness at first hand a different style of classroom management and curriculum delivery and this can be a valuable experience even for the most talented of teachers. Incidental INSET is a natural by-product . . .

Greater differentiation in the delivery of the curriculum and greater differentiation of task/activity can be managed more effectively. It is possible for teachers to try out new approaches; ideas or projects can benefit from the hands-on involvement and continuous evaluation with a fellow professional. A project on the process of writing is currently being developed in this way.

Often staff in a support arrangement settle into a comfortable working relationship where the fact that they find it easy to work together generates all kinds of spin-offs. For this reason it is the practice, if such a relationship develops, to build on it by trying to pair those teachers in future.

D The support teacher resourcing the curriculum

Support time can be made available for resourcing the curriculum. The most efficient and effective way of resourcing the curriculum is for the support teacher to take part in planning the curriculum. This should entail discussion and negotiation *before* resources are prepared so that they are appropriate, rather than – uneconomically – having to be rewritten once they are found to be unsuitable. This avoids providing an 'ambulance service' to an 'ailing curriculum' (Golby and Gulliver, 1979).

It is obviously worthwhile 'banking' any resources which have been prepared to meet students' specific needs. Using this model of support raises questions about how resources are collated and stored departmentally and how other members of the department are made aware of the availability of the materials.

The support teacher can offer advice on the content and the delivery of the curriculum to meet the identified needs of students, and can help to prepare resources. The history key teacher and the modern languages key teacher have also prepared specific course materials using DARTS approaches (Lunzer and Gardner, 1984). Similarly the social studies key teacher has prepared a scheme of work and resources for use with the second year students.

The support teacher can also offer the preparation of supplementary audio/visual/computer resources to meet the needs of specific students, particularly for students with sensory impairment. This support has been improved through the help and specialist advice of the outside support services for students with sensory impairment.

Supplementary materials which are curriculum-based, to develop students' basic skills, can be prepared. For example, the home economics (HE) key teacher has been involved in preparing resources to encourage students to use self help strategies for spelling and yet has used the curriculum content of the HE course.

E The support teacher offering small-scale INSET

Support can be targeted indirectly to meet the needs of the students by being aimed at meeting the needs of the staff and thereby making the curriculum more accessible. The support teacher can help in the preparation of in-service training (INSET) specific to the needs of staff or a department(s) by looking at issues which are broadly considered as relating to 'special needs' and finding strategies which make the process of learning more effective.

For example, as well as INSET for the staff in general on the use of DARTS (Directed Activity Related To Text; Lunzer and Gardner, 1984) specific INSET has been prepared for the science department. In addition INSET which is based on a case study of a particular student, or the difficulties experienced by students with specific needs, can be useful. INSET has also been prepared with the outside support services offering active simulation sessions to staff who teach students with sensory impairment. INSET sessions for careers staff, to raise awareness, are an example of the kind of topics which have been covered. Yet other examples are curriculum-based approaches to spelling, developing writing skills in the context of the curriculum, preparing worksheets or resource materials, meeting the needs of sensory impaired students, difficulties with technical/subject-specific language and developing reading skills in the context of the curriculum.

F The support teacher tracking a student

Monitoring the nature of the curriculum presented to the students and the students' response to that curriculum can be seen as a justifiable use of support time. It can enable staff to identify why a student is having difficulty with the curriculum, or why so little progress is being made.

A report should be written up as a result of the initiative, and a session should be devoted to discussing the outcome of the tracking and the implications for the curriculum within the department.

Making a contract

When the staff in a support relationship have considered the purposes, duration and nature of the support, the nature of the partnership should be discussed so that the teachers concerned are clear about issues such as discipline, resource preparation, marking, assessment and liaison. Finally a support contract is completed and copies given to the head of department concerned and the coordinator (see Figure 12.2).

Support diaries

During the period of support, staff are encouraged to keep support diaries which can be exercise books or loose leaf files. These recordings are meant to be informal and staff are encouraged to make a very personal response. Currently the support teacher and the subject teacher are encouraged to share the diary as an aid to communication. This form of recording draws on Brennan's (1985) suggestion that:

> Teaching records consist of intimate information about the learning of individual students and curriculum presentations in the classroom. They are the working notes of classroom teachers. It is not expected that the notes will be identical in form, for they will reflect the personality, background and professional style of each teacher. Nevertheless they are more than personal notes, and it is essential that the information they contain is made available . . .

Conclusion

The growth of interest in support within the framework of a whole school response has raised many questions; in the future we may see even more radical changes. Once 'remedial' specialists become

Figure 12.2 Support Contract

Copies to: Head of Department and Coordinator

Date:
Name of support teacher:
Name of subject teacher:
Tutor group:
Lesson: Subject:
Agreed duration of support from –   to –
Agreed liaison arrangements:

Names of students (as appropriate)	Students' needs

Purposes of support

How support will be arranged

support teachers what are the consequences for the nature of their intervention?

Should their focus be on 'basic skills'? Should support teachers continue to concentrate on the mechanics of punctuation, computation, reading and the surface structure of the presentation of work? Support teachers need to develop strategies which promote subject learning rather than merely continuing to deliver an 'old' remedial curriculum in a 'new' context. Support and subject teachers need to work together to see how they can develop students' thinking, communication skills, organisational skills, problem-solving strategies and so on.

Subject departments and remedial departments have not always shared the same ideologies, have not always viewed students' learning in the same way; this has not been an issue in the past because there were separate empires for different kinds of students. With the advent of the National Curriculum we need to remind ourselves that this is meant to be a statement of curricular entitlement for *all* students. Perhaps the desire to ensure curricular access for all rather than seek curricular exemption for a few will guarantee the context for the concept and practice of support teaching to flourish.

References

Brennan, W. (1985) *Curriculum for Special Needs*. Milton Keynes: Open University Press.

Buck, M. (1987) 'An Evaluation of a Whole School Approach in a Secondary School'. M. Ed. dissertation, Birmingham University.

Buck, M. (1989) 'Developing a network of support'. *British Journal of Special Education* (in press). See Chapter 7.

Golby, M. and Gulliver, J. R. (1979). 'Whose remedies, whose ills? A critical review of remedial education'. *Journal of Curriculum Studies*, **11**: 137–47.

Lunzer, E. and Gardner, K. (1984) *Learning from the Written Word*. London: Oliver and Boyd.

SECTION 3

Staff Development

At the end of the day the success or failure of a whole school approach will depend upon the attitudes and skills of each teacher within a school. Consequently the issue of staff development is critical. Indeed it can be argued that the first stage in developing a policy for special needs within a school should be to ensure that the special needs of the staff are met. It seems likely that where teachers feel respected, encouraged and recognised for their efforts and achievements, these factors will in turn be reflected in the way the teachers respond to their pupils.

Despite this argument it is sad to note that relatively few articles on the topic of staff development have appeared in the *British Journal of Special Education* in recent years. This is in spite of the fact that the topic has been given particular emphasis by both the Government and local education authorities. Perhaps the publication of this book will stimulate more people to write about their experiences and share their ideas.

We use the term 'staff development' to include a range of processes by which teachers and others can be helped to achieve their professional goals. These include formal courses, in-service workshops, staff meetings, school-based group problem-solving forums and various types of collaborative teaching.

The focus of the chapters in this section is on the question: 'How can staff be provided with help and support?' The contributors make recommendations as to how effective staff development should be more widely achieved. In so doing they reject the use of 'quick-fix' solutions in favour of approaches that emphasise the importance of long-term, coordinated programmes of professional development and support.

In the first chapter in this section David Galloway looks at the implications of a whole school approach for school-focused in-service education. He sees this as an important element in moving from what he calls 'fashionable rhetoric' towards improvements in practice. Jim Muncey and Mel Ainscow provide an account of the early development in one local education authority of an in-service programme that attempts to encourage the idea that all teachers are teachers of children with special educational needs.

At a much more specific level Andy Redpath looks at the staff development needs of teachers engaged in support work. Finally Heather Arthur's chapter describes some of the important outcomes of the evaluation of an in-service course aimed at secondary schools and based on a cascade model. She provides a series of recommendations that are worthy of the attention of all those involved in staff development.

CHAPTER 13

INSET and the Whole School Approach

David Galloway

The Warnock Committee's conclusion, which was endorsed in the 1981 Education Act, that up to 20 per cent of children will have special educational needs at some stage of their school career may be criticised as a statistical artefact resulting from the way in which screening instruments are constructed. It may also be seen as an essentially arbitrary figure, reflecting the committee's view about the proportion of children with learning and/or adjustment difficulties for whom teachers might reasonably require additional help and support. The research on which the committee based the figure of 20 per cent was not new. Indeed, the same conclusion could have been reached on perfectly adequate research evidence at any stage in the previous 50 years (Galloway, 1985a).

Nevertheless, it is clear that teachers frequently see the children concerned as a source of stress. It is also clear that the process of schooling does little for the self esteem of many of these pupils. The achievement of the Warnock Report did not lie in discovering the range and complexity of special educational needs but in opening up debate about appropriate responses at national, local education authority and school levels.

The practical consequences of the extended concept of special educational needs remain, however, unclear. Superficially, the choice lies between a child-focused and a curriculum-focused approach. A child-focused approach emphasises the process of identification and seeks to provide a special programme to meet the identified needs. The programme may involve a wide range of responses, from full time transfer to a special school to additional support in the mainstream. The common element in these responses lies in the underlying assumption that the problem lies with the child: if he or she can be helped to cope with the mainstream curriculum, well and good; if not, we must invoke Warnock's concept of a separate or modified curriculum to justify removal from the mainstream. In contrast, a curriculum-focused approach argues that a curriculum in which as many as 20 per cent of children have special needs must itself be in urgent need of review. This approach takes as its starting point the need to examine whether the school's organisation, curriculum resources and teaching methods enable teachers to cater for the range of needs found in their classrooms.

There is, of course, a problem in practice in this distinction beween a curriculum-focused and a child-focused approach. This is that no curriculum can be taught effectively without recognition of pupils' differing needs, and recognition of differing needs logically implies differential, or special, treatment for some pupils. A curriculum-focused approach does not, therefore, obviate the teacher's responsibility for identifying individual needs. It does, however, mean that special needs are conceptualised as a teaching problem, implying the *teacher's* need to find ways to make the curriculum accessible to the child. The child-focused approach, on the other hand conceptualises special needs as a learning problem, implying the *children's* need for help because of their inability to cope with the curriculum.

Clearly, this distinction will determine the extent to which teachers feel a sense of professional responsibility for pupils with special educational needs. If the need lies in the child then, by implication, neither the curriculum nor their own teaching methods are in need of review. However, this view would not appear to be shared either by Her Majesty's Inspectorate (HMI) or by the Department of Education and Science (DES). In their reports on general inspections of schools, HMI almost invariably comment on provision for pupils with special needs. A heartening trend over the last few years has been the criticism of narrow curricular provision, especially when it occurs in separate classes. There is some evidence that the DES, too, acknowledges the importance of a curriculum-focused approach. In both the first and second years of the new in-service training (INSET) arrangements, training for 'designated' teachers to meet special needs in ordinary schools has been identified as a national priority (DES, 1987). In a subsequent Circular the DES (1988) elaborated on the form it should take. It should aid teachers in:

> identifying impediments to pupils' learning and devising strategies to overcome them;
>
> considering the implications, *for the curriculum and full life of the school as a whole*, of the presence of children with a range of special educational needs;
>
> implementing appropriate forms of organisation for the additional and supplementary help which will give such children *access to the full range of the curriculum* (p. 5) (emphasis added).

There is nothing here about separate or modified curricula. The emphasis is on meeting special needs *within* the mainstream curriculum.

A curriculum-focused approach, then, has implications for all teachers, and hence for all pupils. It is in this sense that it could be described as a 'whole school' approach. For this concept to be credible, we need to spell out what it implies for teachers and for children. We also need to consider how it may be converted from fashionable rhetoric to improved classroom practice.

Implications for teachers and pupils

In her vivid account of slow learners' perceptions of remedial teaching. Simmons (1986) identifies three basic principles in a whole school approach

> that *all* teachers, not just those primarily concerned with special needs, should be aware of the range of needs that might arise in their classrooms;
>
> that *all* teachers should be responsible for assessing the difficulty of materials used in their lessons; and
>
> that *all* teachers should have access to specialised help in dealing, inside the classroom, with children with learning difficulties. (p. 19)

My only reservation about this admirably clear list is that the changing concept of special educational need also requires explicit attention to the rights and responsibilities of pupils. In particular three issues have recurred when the concept of special educational needs is explored on INSET courses:

> ● that *all* pupils should have access to the full range of the curriculum:

- that *all* pupils should have the opportunity, be expected and be seen to contribute usefully to the life and work of the school;
- that *all* pupils, irrespective of ability, should be encouraged to develop an awareness of, and respect for, individual differences.

It is worth noting that the first of these was apparently accepted by the government when it published the Education Reform Bill. The only children who might be exempted from parts of the national curriculum were those with 'statements'. While this exemption clause could be, and was, criticised, it nevertheless seemed probable that the Bill would make it more difficult for secondary schools to offer the academically least able 20 per cent of pupils an alternative, lower-status curriculum. Unfortunately, the government introduced amendments. As a result of these, exemptions may be permitted 'in cases or circumstances' yet to be specified in regulations. Thus, the door is open for children with special needs to continue to be denied access to the mainstream curriculum.

INSET for a whole school approach: some background issues

Introduction: the need for INSET

As envisaged above, a whole school approach will involve a radical programme of development in most schools. This is likely to require a careful evaluation of the education the school is currently offering all its pupils, thus enabling staff to identify priorities. The importance of INSET in this connection can easily be underestimated. It is not something that happens only on designated INSET days (why do so many teachers *insist* on calling them Baker days?). Rather it should be seen as a continuing process in which staff with expertise in a particular area expect, and are expected, to share it with their colleagues. Moreover, INSET is not something which is 'put on' when 'they' (known dismissively in many staff rooms as 'the hierarchy') have decided it is necessary. Rather, the evaluation of current provision is in itself a legitimate and important INSET task.

I would like now to address three issues which have cropped up repeatedly in my own involvement in school-based INSET. The INSET was usually requested by senior staff who hoped to move towards a whole school approach from the starting point of evaluation of what the school was currently offering. It would be easy to identify other issues as equally important. These are given for illustration only because they occurred so frequently.

Academic organisation

As defined above, a whole school approach does not require any particular type of academic organisation. Most primary school children are taught in mixed ability classes. This is probably not so in secondary schools, but a great deal of time and energy can be wasted debating the merits and demerits of different systems, for example mixed ability, banding, setting and streaming.

The research evidence in favour of any one system, either in terms of academic progress or of social relationships, is notoriously limited (Gregory, 1984), not least because the differences between teachers within one system are much greater than the differences between systems. Even in a streamed school, it does not follow that all pupils with special needs will be in the bottom stream. For example, a pupil with specific reading difficulty could be seriously underachieving relative to age and intellectual ability, yet in or near the top stream. Far more important than the formal organisation is the importance teachers attach to their work with exceptional pupils, and the messages that are conveyed to, and about, these pupils, through the hidden curriculum. There is little hard evidence that academic organisation is the determining factor here.

The social climate of the school

A school's social climate is determined as much by its teachers as by its pupil intake. In most schools, moving towards a whole school approach to special educational needs will require a radical shift in orientation with implications for all teachers. The social relationships between groups of staff are likely to be more influential in achieving change, or blocking it, than any aspect of the school's formal organisation. Within every staff there are teachers whose support or opposition can make or break any development. They can include experienced heads of department determined not to be swept along on the latest craze, disillusioned senior teachers who have been passed over for promotion, the active union leader or even the middle-aged person who has so effortlessly collected the coffee money for the last 10 years. For any development to be successful, these undercurrents must be recognised.

In theory, there are two choices: by-pass the people concerned, or find a way to harness their energy by involving them as key figures in part of the programme. In practice, attempts to by-pass critics, leaving them on the sidelines while everyone else gets on with the job, are seldom successful unless the headteacher or programme coordinator is certain of active support from the majority of colleagues. Involving critics in planning and implementing a new project is usually a safer option.

Teachers' job satisfaction

Teaching children with behavioural and/or learning difficulties is potentially the greatest source of stress from day to day classroom teaching. Establishing positive relationships with pupils and seeing them make progress at school are the most important sources of job satisfaction in teaching. It follows that the greater the children's problems, the greater the teacher's sense of achievement when they make progress. This is all very fine in theory but teachers must be forgiven for doubting whether yet another major innovation, on top of everything else that has been imposed in the last few years, will make their work more satisfying rather than still more difficult. Careful thought is needed at the planning stage about the potential benefits for teachers and not just for children. These could include (a) greater understanding and awareness of pupils' needs; (b) easier access to teaching resources and greater skill in using them; (c) help and support from specialist colleagues; (d) new teaching skills, effective in motivating children with a wider range of ability; (e) reduced frustration and stress caused by the children's, and teachers', sense of failure.

Careful thought is also needed about ways to enlist active support from teachers and these are likely to include in-service training. Ward (1976) identifies eight requirements for successful INSET. Staff should feel:

(1)   that the course is their project, and not imposed from outside;
(2)   that it has the wholehearted support of senior staff;
(3)   that it is consistent with their existing ideology (for example in not requiring mixed ability teaching from teachers who are ideologically opposed to this);
(4)   that it does not threaten their autonomy;
(5)   that it is likely to reduce the burden of their work;
(6)   that it gives them a chance to contribute at the planning stage;
(7)   that it involves professional trust and confidence;
(8)   that it is conducted in an open-minded way and allows revision when necessary.

Towards an INSET Programme

One of the first stages in moving towards a whole school approach is to appoint a senior member of staff as coordinator of provision for special needs. Because a whole school approach often requires major changes for all teachers the coordinator must have the ability and authority to break through the inertia that inevitably seeks to maintain the status quo by protecting existing interests. In practice this means that the coordinator should be the headteacher, or in a secondary school perhaps a deputy head, rather than the head of special needs. Less senior staff are unlikely to have the authority to introduce successfully an INSET programme that may have far-reaching implications for all staff. In the early stages it may also be desirable to reflect the changing concept of special educational needs by redefining specialists as members of the learning support team rather than the special needs team.

As implied earlier, planning an INSET programme is itself a valuable form of in-service training. Ideally all staff should be involved in this. In practice the initiative to review existing provision often comes from a group of senior staff. Irrespective of the size of the group, it is striking how enthusiastically and openly most teachers respond to an invitation to examine the process of schooling from the perspective of pupils with special needs. Frequently, they are only too aware of the negative factors which many such pupils experience day by day.

When we start to explore solutions, we have to avoid getting bogged down in fantasies of unlimited time, money, resources and a change of government. The practicality is that school-based INSET is now becoming a realistic possibility. Hence, in planning a whole school approach, an INSET programme over an extended period is feasible.

In Figure 13.1, I identify some of the INSET needs which have emerged at schools in which I have recently acted as 'facilitator' in evaluation of special needs provision. I would emphasise, though, that each school's needs are unique. While I find it hard to envisage a whole school policy operating successfully if the areas identified in Figure 13.1 are not being addressed in *some* way, it is clear that schools will vary widely in their starting point. Elsewhere I have described a school with an apparently successful whole school approach (Galloway, 1985b) but this had developed gradually over a period of years. Whether an INSET programme would contribute to similarly impressive work remains a subject for future inquiry.

Figure 13.1 Developing a whole school approach: priority areas for school-focused INSET over two years

Teacher Groups	Initial INSET Needs
All teachers	Changing concepts of special educational needs (SEN)
Headteacher and coordinators	Management of change within school. Effective uses of LEA support services. Appraisal of work with pupils with SEN
SEN/learning support team	Methods for working with colleagues in mainstream. Methods for developing a resources base. Assessment of SEN within mainstream curriculum.
Heads of department (secondary) and teachers with specific curriculum responsibility (primary)	Promoting colleagues' professional development in relation to SEN pupils. Adapting existing curriculum resources. Development of subject-based resources.
Subject teachers	Assessment of difficulty of materials (eg readability). Selection and use of resources. Assessing/monitoring pupils' progress. Alternative teaching and classroom management strategies.
Pastoral care specialists	Responsibilities of year and form teachers vis à vis pupils with SEN. Review of procedures for parents' liaison. Identifying school's contributions to pupils' behaviour problems.

Conclusions

There are four possible responses to the INSET priority areas identified in Figure 13.1. The first, and perhaps least likely, is broad agreement. The second is that the list is hopelessly incomplete. This may well be true, but no school can allow special needs to monopolise its overall INSET programme and, if the figure identifies too few priority areas, one has to ask how many more could realistically be included. The third is that already far too many priority areas have been included and few schools could sensibly hope to start tackling all of them in one year, or even two. I would dispute this but suggest that, if it is indeed true, then the school should not attempt to move towards a whole school approach and should content itself with more traditional ways of catering for special needs. The fourth possible response to Figure 13.1 is that it identifies the wrong priority areas. This may well be so and it serves to highlight the urgent need for school-based action research on attempts to adopt a whole school approach to special educational needs. A major part of any action research project should focus on the processes involved in planning and carrying out INSET. It needs to go further than this, though. There have so far been few attempts to provide a summative evaluation of school-focused INSET in the area of special educational needs. In other words, we know little about its impact on the subsequent behaviour of teachers and progress of pupils. This is the most difficult kind of evaluation but is necessary if we are not to continue working in the dark.

[This article was first published in *British Journal of Special Education* Vol. 15, No. 4: December 1988.]

References

Department of Education and Science (1987) *LEA Training Grants Scheme 1988-89* (Circular 9(87). London: DES.

Department of Education and Science (1988) *Local Education Authority Training Grants Scheme*: Training to Meet the Special Educational Needs of Pupils with Learning Difficulties in Schools: Guidance Note. (Teacher Training Circular Letter 1/88). DES.

Galloway, D. (1985a) *Schools, Pupils and Special Educational Needs*. London: Croom Helm.

Galloway, D. (1985b) 'Meeting special educational needs in the ordinary school? Or creating them?' *Maladjustment and Therapeutic Education*, **3**, iii: 3-10.

Galloway, D. and Goodwin, C. (1987) *The Education of Disturbing Children*. London: Longman.

Gregory, R. P. (1984) 'Streaming, setting and mixed ability grouping in primary and secondary schools: some research findings'. *Educational Studies*, **10**: 209-226.

Simmons, K. (1986) 'Painful Extractions'. *The Times Educational Supplement*. 17 October.

Ward, J. (1976) 'Behaviour modification in education: an overview and a model for programme implementation'. *Bulletin of the British Psychological Society*, **29**: 257-268.

CHAPTER 14

Launching SNAP in Coventry

James Muncey and Mel Ainscow

All teachers should be teachers of children with special needs. This notion is an obvious consequence of the changes in thinking that have occurred in special education over recent years. Not only is it envisaged that youngsters with more severe disabilities will be increasingly educated in ordinary schools; also in 1978 the Warnock Report recognised that up to 20 per cent of all children have special needs at some time in their school careers (DES, 1978). Teachers must be provided with effective support and training to meet these responsibilities.

In this account we describe Coventry Education Authority's major initiative to help primary school teachers respond to pupils' special needs. The need to make an impact in a large number of schools over a short period and to provide forms of support which are relevant to ordinary class teachers has been foremost in planning the project.

The project

The project is called SNAP (Special Needs Action Programme). It has been developed during the last two years by a group of advisers, special education teachers and educational psychologists. Several features, described below, try to overcome some of the problems frequently associated with in-service education.

Georgiades and Phillimore (1975), for example, suggest that bringing about change in any organisation is very difficult, particularly if it is assumed that changing individuals automatically changes the system. In-service training is tempted to concentrate on importing educational theory into schools with scant regard for the practical skills of the teacher (Olsen, 1982).

Consequently, SNAP attempts to offer practical suggestions based upon sound theoretical principles and stresses strategies for involving all teachers within each school in a positive way.

The aims of SNAP

The project aims:

(1) to encourage headteachers of primary schools to develop procedures for the identification of pupils with special needs;
(2) to assist teachers in primary schools to provide an appropriate curriculum for such pupils;
(3) to coordinate the work of the various special education support services in supporting teachers in primary schools.

These aims are particularly relevant in the light of the 1981 Education Act which requires all schools to develop appropriate procedures for the identification, support and review of pupils with special needs. Faced with this responsibility, local authorities need to develop a coordinated plan – a plan which will provide practical guidance and support to schools, as well as mobilising the resources and support that currently exist to the best advantage. This is what SNAP attempts to achieve.

To understand the development of SNAP, certain aspects of the local context in which it has been formulated must be considered. Coventry is a geographically small area but has a dense population with diverse needs. Special education provision within the city has been generous and an impressive range of facilities and services exists. For a school population of approximately 55,000, there are 15 special schools, several special units and a variety of support agencies working in schools. Furthermore, as a result of Coventry's commitment to in-service education, many of the teachers employed in these schools and services have advanced qualifications.

The changing emphasis in special education calls for wider support from these resources for pupils with special needs in *all* schools. The benefits to both sectors if closer relationships can be developed between ordinary and special schools are also recognised.

A review of existing practice in primary schools suggested that any initiative should attempt to increase teachers' awareness of pupils' special needs and develop their skills in designing and implementing teaching programmes matched to these needs. The following areas, suggested by McCall (1978), provide a useful outline of the issues to be covered:

- assessment, diagnosis and treatment;
- the production of the curriculum and programmes of work to meet the needs of different pupils;
- specialist teaching techniques relevant to children with special needs;
- the way in which support services can be used effectively;
- approaches which enable special and ordinary schools to liaise so that the educational facilities are used to maximum advantage.

SNAP has attempted to encompass these five areas in a practical way which can be used directly by the busy classroom teacher.

Theoretical considerations

A basic philosophy behind the programme has been to look at children in terms of need, rather than to perpetuate the use of categories which, although possibly of some administrative use, have little educational reality. Certainly the research into the consequences of labelling and categorisation suggests that the process is of little direct benefit to the child. Cave and Maddison (1978) point out the process can lower teachers' expectations of what a child can be expected to achieve. Also, focusing on variables outside the direct control of the teacher tends to diminish the responsibility of the teacher in providing appropriate help (Ainscow and Tweddle, 1979). At the very least, the labelling of children implies that they should be treated as a homogeneous group whereas, in terms of the skills that are important for classroom learning, this is far from true (Quay, 1968).

Another key area of SNAP is the early identification of problems, as is stated in the aims of the programme. Many INSET initiatives have begun with formal screening of children (e.g. Gray and Reeve, 1978; Wolfendale, 1976). Because of the inaccuracies in selecting children with learning difficulties by formal testing procedures (Satz and Fletcher, 1979), however, the practice might be thought questionable. Nevertheless, the 1981 Education Act charges education authorities with the responsibility of identifying children with special needs and, once identified, to monitor their progress, If this is to be done efficiently, the class teacher in the ordinary school is crucial to identification and assessment. The teachers' role (Wolfendale and Bryans, 1979) in carrying out assessment is increasingly emphasised; many psychologists recognise that any assessment must be directly related to the curriculum rather than relying on norm-referenced psychometric tests (Cornwall, 1981; Wedell and Lindsay, 1980).

If assessment is related to the curriculum it has the advantage of being of direct practical relevance as well as providing a ready means of regularly checking on a pupil's progress. The use of precisely stated objectives in both assessment and curriculum planning is well documented (Ainscow and Tweddle, 1979), and Cameron (1982) argued that clear objectives, combined with feedback on progress, are a necessary prerequisite for effective teaching. As explained below, one aspect of SNAP is to introduce to teachers the use of objectives in teaching and assessment.

Features of SNAP

One difficulty faced by any local education authority trying to introduce new ideas and techniques to its teaching force is how to do it economically. The 1981 Education Act will require certain practices to be adopted rapidly if all children with special needs are to be identified and then taught efficiently. SNAP has incorporated two ideas, already familiar to in-service educators, in an attempt to change teacher practice.

The first is the identification by the headteacher of people in the school system who have the authority to effect change. These people are designated as coordinators for special needs. They are committed teachers who are fully involved in the school and have the qualities necessary for helping colleagues to learn new approaches. Some heads or deputies have chosen to take personal responsibility for the task. It is the coordinator's role:

- to make colleagues in the school aware of their responsibilities to pupils with special needs;
- to coordinate the development of school-based strategies for the identification, support and review of these pupils;
- to assist teachers in the school in the development of appropriate programmes for these pupils;
- to provide information for colleagues about special education resources and services available in the local authority.

The second feature of SNAP which has been adopted by other in-service initiatives is the use of a 'pyramid-sell' model, so that information and skills can be disseminated as rapidly as possible (McBrien, 1981). This process is initiated by each school's coordinator who is given specialist training in order to become a tutor in his or her own right and disseminate the information amongst colleagues at school. The task of training coordinators in Coventry is made particularly easy by the presence of a flourishing teachers' centre from which numerous in-service courses are run. Thus, coordinators can attend this centre to receive information and attend courses.

In order to disseminate the information and ideas, course materials are produced in a format which enables them to be used in a variety of contexts, including school-based staff training programmes.

To illustrate how this works in practice, a description is given below of the first course to be developed. It is called 'SNAP – Teaching Children with Learning Difficulties'. The way in which the course was developed, and is being evaluated, is described elsewhere (Ainscow and Muncey, 1983).

The learning difficulties course

The SNAP course on learning difficulties is presented in three parts.

Part 1: Introductory session

The first part involves the headteachers of the primary schools, who attend the teachers' centre for one session, during which they are presented with a handbook of information entitled 'Pupils with Special Educational Needs'. The content of the book, which is to be displayed in all staffrooms, includes a description of SNAP; checklists to help identify children with hearing and visual problems; details about the different support agencies, including special schools dealing with different aspects of special educational needs; a bibliography for teachers, parents and children.

During this introductory session, the headteachers are also shown tapes and slides which reinforce the general philosophy behind SNAP and introduce the course on learning difficulties. The tape/slide presentation explains that there are three broad types of special educational needs. First of all, there are children who will require specialist teaching methods; secondly, there are those who require a modified curriculum; and lastly, there are those children who need a supportive environment. It is stressed that the vast majority of children with special educational needs can be supported in ordinary schools.

After this, the action that can be taken is explained briefly with examples of how a curriculum can be adapted to meet the needs of special children, and the way in which the progress of such children can be monitored.

The need to involve parents, and where necessary different support agencies, is also explained. Lastly, the programme that is being offered is introduced. This includes four different aspects – information, courses, materials and support. At the end of the session the need to select an appropriate member of staff to act as coordinator for special needs within their school is stressed.

Part 2: A six-session course

The second part of the programme consists of a six-session course attended by the coordinators from each school. The format of the course is mainly small group discussions and workshop activities led by specially trained teachers from special schools, remedial teachers and educational psychologists. A course manual is provided for participants which contains all the necessary information and materials for the six sessions. Participants are expected to select a child with learning difficulties in their school to form the basis of the case study and they are expected to carry out practical classroom assignments with the child. Central to the approaches presented in the course is a specially designed and field tested basic skills checklist, which teachers use to help them identify children's learning difficulties. Once difficulties are identified, the checklist can be used to help formulate teaching priorities.

Additional information and examples of how the programme works in practice are provided, using video, tape/slide, reading and other materials.

The people who act as tutors must have successfully completed a course themselves. As tutors they are not required to give lectures or provide extra theoretical information. Instead their main goals are:

● to involve all participants in full discussion of the course materials;
● to ensure that participants understand the tasks they are to carry out;
● to nurture a positive attitude amongst participants towards overcoming children's learning difficulties;

A 70-page tutors' guide is provided which includes general advice on working with groups, dealing with problems and encouraging discussion. Specific instructions are given on the timing of each session and the issues which are to be emphasised. In addition, the guide contains a selection of further reading.

Part 3: Liaison and follow-up

After completion of the six-session course, part three of the programme begins. Evidence from other in-service initiatives has indicated the importance of systematic follow up if change is to be sustained. Consequently, follow up is provided using a combination of remedial teachers, educational psychologists, advisers and teachers from special schools. In addition, each primary school is attached to a named special school, which has trained tutors on the staff. This is expected to promote the exchange of information between ordinary and special schools, whilst also encouraging the special schools to become special educational resource centres, as suggested in the Warnock Report.

Two other strategies are employed at this stage. Firstly, co-ordinators write up their case studies carried out on the course. These are published in book form and distributed to course members to act as a continued source of ideas on programming planning. Course participants who successfully complete a case study are awarded a course certificate, which enables them to act as course tutors for further courses. Secondly, at the end of the course each school is visited by an adviser who discusses with the headteacher the formulation of a school-based policy for children with special needs, and the options for a school-based follow-up. These options are:

(1)   to run an awareness meeting for staff using the tape/slide presen-
      tations, and other material;
(2)   to mount a full six-session course for staff using the multi-media
      package which was presented to the coordinators at the teachers'
      centre;
(3)   to work with individual members of staff as suggested in stage
      two of the assessment of special needs outlined in the Warnock
      Report;
(4)   to arrange meetings with parents which might include presen-
      tation of the tape/slide material, distribution of further infor-
      mation, and so on.

In addition, headteachers are invited to attend a further meeting during which they are expected to present the policy that their school has adopted.

Many schools have decided initially to run an awareness meeting for staff and then either to work with individual members of staff or mount a full six-session course. As the latter option is a major undertaking some schools have had to delay this until they have reorganised their priorities for school-based in-service training. We are currently preparing another short package which will illustrate some of the different approaches adopted by schools, so that other schools embarking on the programme will have the benefit of colleagues' experience and be provided with good models.

Further developments

The course on learning difficulties is the first to have been developed for the Special Needs Action Programme. As such, it also provides a means of establishing the coordinator's role in each primary school. Further courses are currently being developed, as can be seen in Figure 14.1, which illustrates how these relate to one another. A brief description of these and other packages is given below.

Daily measurement

This is a self contained, multi-media package which can be delivered in four $1\frac{1}{2}$-hour sessions. It extends some of the techniques and ideas introduced in the learning difficulties course, as well as being a prerequisite for the course on using DATA-PAC described below.

DATA-PAC

This stands for 'Daily Teaching and Assessment: Primary Aged Children' and consists of materials to help teachers devise individualised programmes for pupils with learning difficulties. The package, which was originally developed by a team of educational psychologists seconded to Birmingham University, also provides suggestions for teaching methods and a means of monitoring progress (Akerman et al., 1983). It is being adapted to make it compatible with other SNAP materials.

128

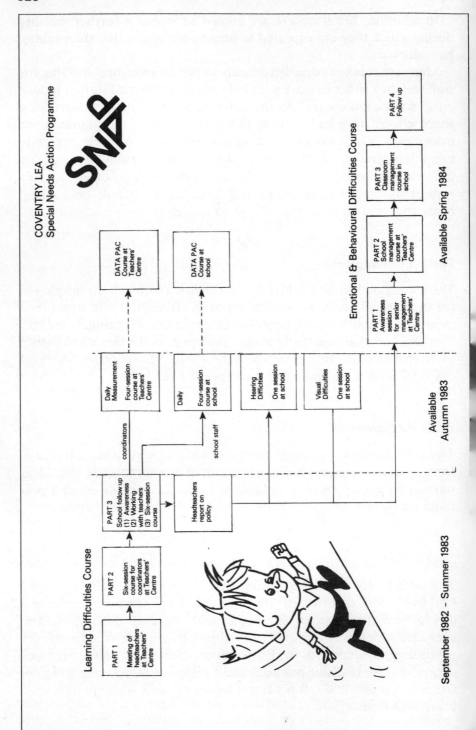

Hearing difficulties

This consists of a tape/slide presentation and a short booklet, and can be delivered in one session. It deals with the identification and support of children with hearing difficulties.

Visual difficulties

This tape/slide presentation on the education of children with visual difficulties is now available. In addition, the working party which has developed this is investigating the possibility of producing further in-service material dealing with this area in greater depth.

Emotional and behavioural problems

In September 1982 a working party was established to examine ways in which teachers could be helped to support pupils with emotional and behavioural problems. A four-part, in-service course is likely to be available shortly. The first part will be an awareness session for senior members of staff who will then be invited to take part in a course on school management implications. This will lead to an optional, school-based course about classroom management. Finally, schools will be expected to report back on the policy decisions made as a result of course participation.

In providing this range of courses, the intention is to ensure that all class teachers are helped to meet the needs of all children in their classes. Furthermore, the involvement of the coordinators in disseminating these courses will increase their skills and strengthen their roles within the schools' organisational framework.

SNAP in the schools

At the time of writing, SNAP has been introduced to over 70 primary schools in Coventry and the remainder will be taking part in the course during the school year which has just begun. An in-depth evaluation is being completed by a team of researchers from Leicester University and will be published but only time will tell what are the full implications and effects of the initiative. Nevertheless, it is interesting to consider some of the activities carried out by schools that have taken part.

The emphasis within the programme is on getting the staff of each school to use the course materials in order to review existing procedures and to create a policy for meeting special needs. Consequently individual schools are likely to develop different policies according to pupils' needs, the curriculum and the organisation's constraints.

In one inner city junior school, for example, where a relatively large proportion of children have special needs, the headteacher has established 'SNAG' – the Special Needs Action Group. This consists of the various support personnel available, i.e. the coordinator for special needs, who happens to be the deputy head, a part time 'remedial' teacher, a multicultural specialist and the educational psychologist attached to the school. Class teachers are required, at least annually, to refer to SNAG any child whose progress is causing concern. After an assessment of the child's needs, the team discusses with the class teacher the range of support responses that are to be made. Whilst various forms of help and advice may be provided, the team emphasises that the class teacher retains overall responsibility for the child's progress.

An open plan primary school in a residential area of the city has chosen to develop a central resource area housing materials for supporting pupils with special needs. The headteacher has elected to take on the role of coordinator herself and she is concentrating on establishing suitable procedures for identifying and defining pupils' areas of need. She helps individual teachers to formulate suitable teaching programmes and monitor progress. Given the nature of the building and the school commitment to team teaching, this seems to be an appropriate strategy for supporting teachers and pupils.

In another inner city school, with over 80 per cent of children from minority backgrounds, there has been a long tradition of part time specialist teachers who withdrew 'problem' children for special attention in small groups. The headteacher and her coordinator felt that this type of approach was no longer appropriate, particularly as it seemed to have encouraged some class teachers to assume that others would take responsibility for dealing with children's difficulties. In establishing the role of the coordinator, therefore, help for children in their own classrooms and constant participation of the class teacher have been emphasised. This orientation was established initially by getting all members of staff to participate in the SNAP learning difficulties course on site, each designing and implementing an individual teaching programme with one child in the class.

An encouraging common feature of these accounts of using SNAP is the clear emphasis in all three schools on class teachers retaining responsibility for the progress and welfare of all children in their class.

Conclusion

One of the major problems that has arisen is that the onerous tasks required of the coordinators have possibly been underestimated. If any beneficial change is to be brought about in schools the coordinator must be given considerable support. This has necessitated a great deal of administrative work as every effort has been made to keep all the support services in the city up to date with the developments in the programme. Until Easter no specific time was allocated for work attached to the programme, although during the course of the summer term one of the writers was seconded to work on SNAP two days a week and this secondment is likely to continue for a further year.

Despite such difficulties our experience in working with the schools that have participated in SNAP so far leads us to believe that the overall effect has usually been a positive one. Several features seem to encourage changes within schools and deserve consideration by others attempting to implement similar projects. These are described below.

☐ SNAP recognises the need for teachers to play a central role in identifying and meeting educational needs, as recommended in various government reports (e.g. DES, 1975; DES, 1978). Since research suggests that teachers are well able to predict which children have learning problems (Keogh and Smith, 1970; Kapelis, 1975), attention is given to helping teachers assess children in terms of competencies needed to progress effectively within a particular classroom (Eaves and McLaughlin, 1977) and in relation to a particular curriculum.

☐ A structure is given for following the five stages of assessment outlined in the Warnock Report. This is compatible with the requirements of the 1981 Education Act, which requires schools to identify and provide appropriate support for children with special educational needs. In addition, SNAP coordinates the work of the different support agencies and establishes closer links between ordinary and special schools in order to promote the exchange of ideas, materials and personnel.

☐ All course materials are designed for use in a variety of contexts, including school-based staff development programmes. All the staff in a school can take an active role in the teacher training programme, while the concept of special education as an extension of ordinary school placement is promoted (McCarthy, 1972).

☐ A key member of staff is designated as coordinator and acts as a change agent within each school (Georgiades and Phillimore, 1975). As the coordinator can then act as tutor, this promotes the pyramid-sell model of in-service work, which enables large numbers of teachers to be influenced over a short period.

☐ The SNAP courses are practical and use a competency based approach with clearly stated objectives for participants, indicating skills, knowledge and attitudes to be developed (Blackhurst, 1977). The practical experience gained by participants is regarded as crucial and this aspect of the programme is well regarded by teachers (Siegal, 1969). In addition, the tutors are practising teachers or educational psychologists who have themselves successfully completed the course.

Readers interested in purchasing SNAP course materials should send for further details from Elm Bank Teachers' Centre, Mile Lane, Coventry CV1 2LQ.

[This article was first published in *Special Education: Forward Trends* Vol. 10, No. 3: September 1983.]

References

Ainscow, M. and Tweddle, D. A. (1979) *Preventing Classroom Failure: An Objectives Approach*. Chichester: Wiley.

Ainscow, M. and Muncey, J. (1983) *Learning Difficulties in the Primary School: An In-Service Training Initiative*. Coventry: LEA.

Akerman, T., Gillet, D., Kenwood, P., Leadbetter, P., Mason, L., Matthews, C., Tweddle, D. A. and Winteringham, D. (1983) 'DATA-PAC – an interim report'. Submitted to the *AEP Journal*.

Blackhurst, A. E. (1977) 'Competency-based Education Personnel Preparation'. In Kneedler R. D. and Tarver S. G. (eds.), *Changing Perspectives in Special Education*. Columbus, Ohio: Merrill.

Cameron, R. J. (1982) 'Teaching and evaluating curriculum objectives'. *Remedial Education*, **17**, (3): 102–108.

Cave, D. and Maddison, P. (1978) *A Survey of Recent Research in Special Education*. Slough: NFER.

Cornwall, K. F. (1981) 'Some trends in pupil evaluation: the growing importance of the teacher's role'. *Remedial Education*, **16**, (4): 157–161.

Department of Education and Science (1975) *A Language for Life* (The Bullock Report). London: HMSO.

Department of Education and Science (1978) *Special Educational Needs* (The Warnock Report). London: HMSO.

Eaves, R. C. and McLaughlin, P. (1977) 'A systems approach for the assessment of the child and his environment: getting back to basics'. *Journal of Special Education*, **11**: 99–111.

Georgiades, N. J. and Phillimore, L. (1975) 'The Myth of the Hero-innovator and Alternative Strategies for Organisational Change'. In Kiernan C. C. and Woodford F. P. (eds.) *Behaviour Modification for the Severely Retarded*. Amsterdam: Associated Scientific.

Gray, D. and Reeve, J. (1978) 'Ordinary schools: some special help'. *Special Education: Forward Trends*, 5, (1): 25–27.

Kapelis, L. (1975) 'Early identification of reading failure: a comparison of two screening tests and teacher forecasts'. *Journal of Learning Disabilities*, 8: 638–641.

Keogh, B. K. and Smith, C. (1970) 'Early identification of educationally high potential and high risk children'. *Journal of School Psychology*, 8: 285–290.

McBrien, J. (1981) 'Introducing the EDY project'. *Special Education: Forward Trends*, 8, (2): 29–30.

McCall, C. (1978) 'Implications of the Warnock Report for teachers and teacher-training: a brief review and suggested reading'. *Remedial Education*, 13, (4): 173–187.

McCarthy, J. M. (1972) *A Legacy of Service: A Commitment to Excellence*. Florida State Department of Education: Education for Exceptional Children Section.

Olsen, T. P. (1982) 'School-based in-service education: model or Utopia?' *British Journal of In-Service Education*, 8, (2): 73–79.

Quay, H. (1968) 'The facets of educational exceptionality: a conceptual framework for assessment, grouping and instruction'. *Exceptional Children*, 35: 25–31.

Satz, P. and Fletcher, J. M. (1979) 'Early screening tests, some uses and abuses'. *Journal of Learning Disabilities*, 12, (1): 56–59.

Siegal, E. (1969) *Special Education in the Regular Classroom*. New York: John Day.

Wedell, K. and Lindsay, G. A. (1980) 'Early identification procedures: what have we learned?' *Remedial Education*, 15, (3): 130–135.

Wolfendale, S. (1976) 'Screening and early identification of reading and learning difficulties. A description of the Croydon screening procedures'. In Wedell K. and Raybould E. C. (eds.) *The Early Identification of Educationally 'At Risk' Children*. Birmingham: School of Education, Birmingham University.

Wolfendale, S. and Bryans, T. (1979) *Identification of Learning Difficulties – A Model of Intervention*. Staffs: National Association for Remedial Education.

CHAPTER 15

Skills for Successful Support

Andy Redpath

It is a subject of continuing debate among historians as to whether outstanding personalities impose their will upon events or events themselves are the product of deeper, more powerful forces. In some respects the issue of integration for children with special educational needs poses similar questions. Will a pupil's opportunity for an integrated education be largely affected by policy statements from national government and local education authorities? Or is it more likely to be realised if certain key individuals possess the necessary skills as well as the commitment and other personal qualities to make it work? Clearly both are essential ingredients for successful integration. However it is only recently that courses for teachers on special educational needs have given sufficient attention to the training requirements of those doing support work.

This chapter discusses some of the new skills which need to be acquired by support teachers, in order that they can contribute positively to the policy of integration. It also suggests that those giving classroom support may need to possess certain personal qualities if these skills are to be successfully acquired and put into practice.

The Warnock Report (1978) recognised the importance of offering help to classroom teachers, if pupils with special educational needs were to be successfully integrated into mainstream schools. It was envisaged that existing remedial staff would form the basis of a new, unified support service. This often means a fundamental change in long established methods of working, moving away from the practice of withdrawing pupils for individual tuition and, instead, concentrating on offering support to both teachers and children in the classroom.

Thus, one of the challenges facing those involved in support work is how to transfer expertise gained from working at the child level and make it more generally available to colleagues throughout the wider school. This is no easy task, particularly since, quite naturally, teachers often resent being told what to do by so-called 'experts' from outside. Seemingly good ideas may be politely listened to, but that in itself is no guarantee they will be acted upon.

What follows is based on the author's evaluation, in the summer of 1988, of the work of a teacher based at a school for children with emotional and behavioural difficulties in an urban borough. The teacher had established a support service in two local primary schools in September 1987. The evaluation included interviews with staff, parents and educational psychologists, the distribution of a question-naire to the teachers at both schools, and the introduction of an exercise with two classes to gauge the perceptions of children.

Limited evidence from this case study suggests that a support teacher can help effect wider school change. However, the success of support services offering advice to teachers in what many see as a private domain – the classroom – is inextricably linked with the per-sonal skills of the provider. That support teachers have to work with tact and sensitivity, in sometimes difficult circumstances, underlines the importance of developing appropriate skills.

The support teacher needs to build a credible presence among staff in the host school, gaining acceptance by fostering mutual pro-fessional development and respect. This is particularly important when the teacher is trying to move away from the 'withdrawal model' still favoured by many teachers. Davies and Davies (1988) have listed several interdependent factors instrumental in establishing credibility and sustaining it. Four were particularly relevant to the success of the support service discussed in this chapter: consultation and negotiation, positive professional exchange, responsive and flexible approaches, and humour and perspective. To these, four others emerged during the course of the study which can be profitably added: rapport with children, 'ownership' of change, sensitivity to 'micro-political' pro-cesses, and counselling skills. This is not intended as a definitive list; rather it is suggested that an awareness of some of these skills and qualities could prove useful to teachers concerned with providing support.

It is important to stress that the support teacher in this particular study had many years' experience of working with children who were displaying behavioural difficulty, both at a special school and in helping to integrate them into mainstream schools.

Consultation and negotiation

The support teacher himself stressed the need to seek teachers' views and negotiate a course of action with them. It was important to listen to colleagues, recognise their perceptions as valid and empathise with their problems. This process of consultation was extended to children whom the support teacher felt were not always aware of teacher expectations or the consequences of their own behaviour.

Positive professional exchange

A specific 'problem-solving' approach was adopted which encouraged the class teacher and support teacher to tackle a mutual problem together. Emphasising that he was 'joining with' teachers, the support teacher deliberately referred to 'us' or 'we' when describing a problem or discussing its possible solution with a teacher. He felt it was important to build mutual respect and 'hold back on instant solutions'.

Responsive and flexible approaches

There was an emphasis on working from the teacher's position, and having a 'feel for the situation' existing in the classroom. It was apparent that teachers were more favourably inclined towards change that builds on existing practice (as in the Special Needs Action Programme, Coventry). Teaching styles are essentially personal and different. Through an understanding of the nuances of the teaching process and the enhancing of it, progress was more likely to be made.

Humour and perspective

Staff in both schools looked forward to the support teacher coming in and spoke warmly about him in his absence. He had established a highly visible presence, based upon humour and 'jokey informality' in dealing with colleagues. Several teachers felt that the success of the project was largely due to the support teacher's amenable and jovial personality. 'He cheers me up when I feel frustrated,' commented one headteacher.

Rapport with children

A common complaint among teachers is that those who offer advice frequently 'cannot do the job themselves' or are 'no good with kids'. The support teacher's obvious ability to communicate well with children was central to teachers' recognition of his skills, respect for his judgement and acceptance of his advice. Casually acknowledging children around the school, engaging them in conversation and offering praise and encouragement were essential features of his approach, which aided children in developing a positive self image. Popularity with the children, based upon respect, allowed classroom intervention by the support teacher to be an enriching experience, rather than a disruptive one which brought with it new problems of discipline and control. In short, acceptance by pupils encouraged the development of a positive class teacher/support teacher relationship.

Encouraging ownership of change

The support teacher said, 'It is not enough to say what is wrong. Involving teachers in a process of change is important to make it last or stick.' Developing this theme, Dessent (1987) has referred to the need for ordinary schools and teachers to 'own' their problems and solutions. Writing about the implementation of SNAP, Muncey and Ainscow (1983) have stressed the need for teachers to feel they are involved in defining problems and formulating solutions; then they are more likely to implement any changes agreed. Recognising this approach, the support teacher emphasised that selling solutions, however worthy, was not constructive. 'You must not try to impose ideas and become involved in battles you cannot win.'

Sensitivity to 'micro-political' processes

Hoyle (1982) has referred to the existence in schools of micro-political processes, whereby individuals and groups informally exert influence on decision-making. This is characterised 'more by coalitions than by departments, by strategies rather than by enacted rules, by influence rather than by power, and by knowledge rather than by status'. Recognising this perspective, the support teacher stressed the need to 'stand back and be observant' and be wary of 'identifying with particular factions or groups in schools'. To do so would 'restrict the ability to negotiate with a variety of people'.

By maintaining circumspection and distance, the support teacher achieved informal acceptance in both staffrooms and gained respect from the broad spectrum of staff existing in the two schools.

Counselling skills

The above factors may best be viewed as interdependent 'elements'. Underpinning them all, and perhaps fundamental to the success of the project, were the skills of an effective counsellor.

In relation to the personality of a successful counsellor, Hamblin (1974) has stressed some important qualities. The first is 'empathy' or the ability to 'feel into' a person or situation. Hamblin states that this is more than an intellectual exercise; it is a 'type of momentary identification'. Second come 'spontaneity and genuineness', the capacity to relate honestly and reveal oneself as 'one human being to another'. Linked with this, it seems necessary to possess a feeling of self worth. Finally, the counsellor must have the capacity to show a 'non-threatening, safe and non-possessive warmth'. The support teacher's acceptance in the classroom and staffroom of each school was in large part due to his ability to listen to colleagues, show empathy, demonstrate warmth and genuineness, build on their ideas and encourage them to seek solutions within their own capabilities. Staff at both schools valued his company, regarding him as having a sympathetic ear and as someone with whom they could talk freely and openly.

Conclusion

An attempt has been made to unravel some of the personal qualities and skills which have aided the success of one particular support service. It would seem that the skills necessary for this 'counselling' role are quite different from those traditionally employed by teachers working with children withdrawn from the classroom for individual help. The redeployment of existing staff, as envisaged by the Warnock Report, may not always prove to be a realistic option. Teachers entering schools and classrooms to offer support and advice need to be aware of a sophisticated range of approaches, which has implications for staff recruitment and training. Perhaps local education authorities need to concentrate more on the quality of personnel rather than simply increasing the numbers of teachers providing support.

This may seem a tall order. However, if these new skills are acquired in some measure, and put to effective use among teachers generally, an atmosphere of mutual cooperation and trust can flourish. Where this prevails, staff are likely to do more than simply listen to new ideas. They will develop their own professional skills and resources, making the whole school approach to special educational needs a more realistic prospect.

Thus, there is some evidence to suggest that, for a policy of integration to become a practical reality, it does need to be implemented by responsive and suitably trained personnel.

References

Davies, J. D. and Davies, P. (1988) 'Developing credibility as a support and advisory teacher'. *Support for Learning*, 3: 12–15.
Dessent, T. (1987) *Making the Ordinary School Special*. Lewes: Falmer Press.
Hamblin, D. H. (1974) *The Teacher and Counselling*. Oxford: Blackwell.
Hoyle, E. (1982) 'The micropolitics of educational organisation'. *Educational and Management Administration*, 10: 87–98.
Muncey, J. and Ainscow, M. (1983) 'Launching SNAP in Coventry'. *Special Education: Forward Trends*, 10, 3: 8–12 (see Chapter 14).

CHAPTER 16

INSET Issues and Whole School Policies

Heather Arthur

A whole school approach to special educational needs and its underlying belief that a student's individual learning problems in any subject are that teacher's responsibility is a long way from the notion that students with learning difficulties are best taught individually, or in small groups, by a remedial specialist away from the stress of the mainstream curriculum. Although it now sounds somewhat extreme, the second of those approaches to special needs provision is by no means unknown, even in this post-Warnock, post-81 Act era.

The developing role of the special needs coordinator has, in many schools, helped to bridge the gap between these philosophies, enabling children with learning difficulties to integrate more readily with their mainstream peers. However, this development does not automatically guarantee access to the full curriculum unless all teachers in a school recognise their responsibility in making specialist teaching available to all students in an appropriately differentiated form.

This chapter looks at an in-service project undertaken by a local education authority (LEA) in order to encourage a sense of shared responsibility for special needs by its secondary teachers and thus to foster the LEA's whole school approach policy to special needs in schools by means of in-service training (INSET). It then highlights some of the lessons learned from the evaluation of the project (Arthur, 1988). A brief description of the nature of the evaluation and of the course is given first.

The evaluation

The evaluation of the pilot project was conducted in two parts: the first considered the in-service section and the related materials; the second attempted to assess the implementation phase of the course and its effects on the schools taking part. Data for the first part was gathered from rapid response questionnaires completed at the end of each session by course participants, from focused interviews with the link teachers conducted in their schools and by the evaluator attending the course as a participating observer. The data for the second part was gathered from focused interviews conducted in schools over a period of time and from a questionnaire designed to assess the level of development of a whole school approach.

The evaluation, conducted over 15 months, was designed to end one year after the completion of the INSET phase of the course. While it would obviously be too early to see all the course's aims being achieved – Fullan (1982) suggests three to five or more years are needed for implementation and institutionalisation – the study could continue only for a limited time. Three terms after the INSET phase, when a new school year would be well underway, seemed a reasonable point at which to end the evaluation period. Formative feedback was given to the LEA throughout.

The in-service process

A cascade model for the LEA was adopted, with seven secondary schools in a first year pilot programme and other secondary schools in stages, as the course was repeated.

The course used was 'Special Needs in the Secondary School: A Whole School Approach', produced as part of the Special Needs Action Programme (SNAP) by Coventry LEA. Its aims are 'to develop positive attitudes towards the idea of meeting special educational needs in the secondary school; to assist schools in reviewing their policies and practices with regard to special needs; and to provide information about available support services and the implications of the 1981 Education Act'. The intended long term outcomes are that 'the school should have reviewed its arrangements for meeting special educational needs; individual departments should have reviewed their curriculum, teaching methods and resources to question their appropriateness for all pupils; all teachers should have reviewed their present practice and reached the stage when they have ideas about what to do next and all staff should be aware of what help and support are available within the Local Authority' (extracts from the course advertisement).

The course itself operates on a cascade model by training two teachers from each school, known as 'Link Teachers', for six INSET sessions. On return to their schools they are intended to involve all their staff in a school-based initiative, building on what they learnt on the course and working towards a whole school approach. Participants are intended to have a high status within their schools and most schools were represented by a deputy head and special needs co-ordinator.

The INSET sessions and related written materials deal with: key issues, curriculum, school organisation, classroom organisation and practice, attitudes and relationships, support and help. One of these topics is dealt with at each session and is supported by pre-session reading.

The evaluation found the course to be sophisticated in design and soundly based on the findings of modern educational research related to special needs, to the change process, to INSET design and to the way in which teachers learn. The course is designed to operate in three phases:

(1) Preparation (designed to achieve support for the link teachers during the implementation phase from heads, advisers, educational psychologists and governors);
(2) INSET;
(3) School based initiatives.

In reality, a fourth phase, *implementation*, must be recognised as crucial to the change initiative. A major feature of the course is the high quality written materials provided to cover each session. These consist of background reading, tutor notes and resources. They are presented in sections at each INSET session and not *en bloc* at the start of the course. The INSET sessions themselves are multi-media, multi-topic and presented in a lively but thought provoking way. Discussion is carefully structured by means of constantly changing groups. The materials are designed to be ready for use in school in the cascade process or they can be adapted to meet particular needs.

A high level of satisfaction with the course was recorded by members both in the rapid response questionnaires and when interviewed. Yet by the end of phase 3, the school-based initiative, little that was directly related to the course had been achieved. At the whole day session held at the end of this phase (three months after the INSET) schools reported on what they had undertaken.

Only one school had been able to begin the kind of cascade process envisaged by the course and that was because it already had regular, weekly timetabled, INSET sessions which had been achieved by adjusting the timetable so that students went home early one afternoon each week. (This mechanism enabled the school to continue INSET and meetings throughout the whole period of industrial action.) Other course members had undertaken activities such as testing reading levels, writing a staff booklet or identifying areas of particular needs but these were activities which, although relevant, were not specifically course-related. This is a far from uncommon phenomenon, perhaps, in in-service training but if we are to accept that 'the extent to which professional development activities succeed is the extent to which change succeeds' (Fullan, 1982) then the reasons for failure to implement need to be analysed and acted upon.

Issues arising from the pilot course

In fairness, it must be noted that the pilot course fell partly in the period of industrial action and was inevitably affected by it. However, there is general agreement by those who took part that the points which are made here are equally relevant to 'normal' times.

The issues fall into three main categories: the cascade process; problems arising from success; and the need for support. I will identify each of these briefly in turn and then summarise some of the major lessons learned from the project.

1   The cascade model in in-service training

The use of a cascade model to implement change makes a number of assumptions, not the least of which is that 'the message' can or will remain intact throughout the process, even if that process is not followed exactly as the course designer intended. The evaluation period in this study did not continue long enough to assess this formally but it seems fairly clear, from what is happening in a number of schools now, that the message appears to have shifted from that of 'all teachers should have an insight into special needs and review their practices' to one of 'there should be a support teacher in the classroom to assist students with special needs'. This may be regarded as a definite move in the right direction, in that it gives students with special needs greater access to the curriculum, but it still allows a subject teacher or department to remain dependent on someone else and to avoid any responsibility themselves.

However, the two assumptions most relevant to this study are those associated with the suitability of the 'cascader' for the task and those associated with time. In the case of the first, those selected to attend the course and to be trained as trainers need not only sufficient status in their schools but also the respect of their staff in order to influence and bring about a whole school approach through INSET, guidance and catalytic enthusiasm. However, it needs to be remembered that not all deputy heads or heads of special needs are automatically endowed with these qualities and a head who wants a change initiative to succeed in his school needs to bear this in mind and to select with care.

Two principal assumptions are about time factors in a cascade process: firstly that 'cascaders' have time to plan and implement their initiatives and secondly that staff have the time to be 'cascaded'. The reality is that those likely to be the trainers in a cascade process will also have other major responsibilities in school as well as their teaching commitments. They will, therefore, have little time to plan efficiently, organise speakers, arrange INSET or support colleagues in order to make the training work effectively. Similarly, few schools are structured to enable a cascade process to take place without separate planning and organisation for it. Grant related in-service training (GRIST) funding and designated in-service days ('Baker Days') now make this process much easier but, with all the many demands on these, the time when the cascade in-service will take place still needs to be identified and planned for well in advance.

2 Problems arising from success

A successful outcome of the course is that teachers will want to cater for special educational needs in their own subject. That will usually lead to requests for help with the adaptation and preparation of materials; with developing appropriate methodologies; with developing the role of support teachers and widening that of special needs co-ordinators; with developing school policies for things like spelling and work presentation; with ways of increasing pupil motivation and involvement and with the development of resource centres. Such requests will need to be catered for and may require further INSET. In this pilot the requests for further INSET ranged from 54 to 71 per cent of staff in the schools involved.

Other 'problems' arising from success will be the need to recognise and 'manage' the inevitable feelings of insecurity and of being deskilled which teachers often feel when they attempt to change their practices. At the school level, recognition of the need to change policies and practices may call for changes to the timetable and curriculum structure or may highlight the hidden messages in displays, extra-curricular activities and school publications. The implications of success are clearly far reaching and will make demands on all aspects of school life.

3   The need for support

The need for support is recognised by the course and catered for in the preparation phase. Not surprisingly, however, it did not turn out as intended and it would be naive to assume that it would. Advisers are already overloaded. Headteachers have so many demands upon them that it is difficult to keep one initiative in high focus among so many other, and often more pressing, ones. Governors are generally still a long way from fully understanding their responsibilities in this area. The support which educational psychologists can offer is influenced by their caseload, personal interests and their existing relationship with their schools.

Yet the need for support in the implementation phase is crucial as Fullan (1982), Hopkins (1986), Joyce and Showers (1980) all emphasise. Heads and senior management need opportunities to examine the implications of the change and to consider new approaches. They need the support of someone who, as well as being deeply committed to the development of a whole school approach, has a clear grasp of secondary school structures and management issues – someone who can overcome blockages caused or excused by curriculum inertia and timetable constraints by stimulating ideas for new approaches and by encouraging the confidence to try them.

Link teachers need the support of someone who fully understands the course and its aims, who will talk through and suggest ways of overcoming the difficulties being experienced and who will have the time to arrange speakers and help to organise INSET sessions which the link teacher is unlikely to have. Link teachers also need the support which comes from discussion and the opportunity to share successes and failures with their counterparts in other schools so that they do not become disheartened but have the benefit of shared counsel and experience to overcome any feelings of isolation if colleagues in their schools do not share their philosophy.

The classroom practitioners, as already indicated, need a great deal of support at this time. They need the opportunity for philosophical discussion as they examine their attitudes and teaching practices. They need the support of someone who will act as a catalyst in generating new ideas and who will not undermine the confidence gained from what they have successfully done in the past but will build on this to inspire confidence as new ideas are tried and tested. Not least, they need practical help from someone who is a respected practitioner who will work alongside them to demonstrate, support or experiment in the classroom or to take over the class on occasions so that the teacher has time to plan strategies and produce new or revised materials.

All of these needs for support could have been met in ideal circumstances by the intended support structure but ideal circumstances seldom, if ever, exist in the realms of education. The question must be: if support is crucial to the successful implementation of a course, how can this support be provided. If the LEA is not committed to providing it then there is little point in incurring the expense of the course in the first place. Enough is now known about what makes for successful INSET – Rudduck (1981), Fullan (1981, 1985), Hopkins (1986) – for course planners to recognise that support has got to be built in from the start.

In recognition of these levels of need for support, the LEA appointed a professional development tutor whose role is similar to that of an advisory teacher in some local authorities. At the time of the pilot, this appointment was a one-year, full time secondment from a school to work with the presentation of the course to the next group of schools. In addition she was also able to offer some support to the pilot phase. The teacher seconded was a highly regarded special needs co-ordinator whose philosophy was very much in tune with that of the course. She had a perceptive understanding of management systems and curriculum organisation as well as extensive experience in special educational provision. This background, and a personal confidence which inspired the confidence of others, made it possible for her to support all three levels of need, senior management, link teachers and individual classroom teachers, in developing their strategies for a whole school approach to special needs.

Throughout the time of her appointment, she worked with the pilot schools by assisting discussions to create supportive curriculum structures; providing in-service training on compulsory in-service days; supporting individual teachers by generating ideas or demonstrating classroom strategies and by offering formative feedback to the

LEA to inform the planning of the second presentation of the course. Her influence, coupled with the introduction of directed time and compulsory in-service days, enabled the schools to make progress with the cascade process which had not been possible before.

Some lessons learned from the project

Issues have emerged which, though not new, may be so obvious as to be easily overlooked when change is planned. Structured planning may be an essential prerequisite for success. Planning beyond the structured in-service stage obviously carries resource implications which may be why it is so often minimised or even disregarded. Yet the resource implications need not be prohibitive if they are planned and built in from the start. It is, after all, illogical to spend money on in-service training if that training has little opportunity to be translated into practice. Let us look at some ways in which the planning could be improved at the LEA and the school level.

At the LEA level

A clear understanding of the nature and process of the course is essential so that this can be conveyed to all those interested in taking part. It is not enough to invite heads to send representatives to the INSET: the long term implications for the school must be explained to and accepted by the head and a commitment to plan for and support these when the INSET phase is finished must be given. Some kind of contractual arrangement might not be inappropriate in certain circumstances.

Another implication for the LEA is a commitment to support the school-based phase in workable, practical ways. The method will vary according to the support structures which already exist in a local authority. What is clear is that it is not enough to expect overloaded advisers to provide the kind of support which was identified earlier. Someone needs to be given direct responsibility for this support, to ensure that it materialises. A network for link teachers from the schools involved would also provide a supportive mechanism and give them an opportunity to exchange ideas and assist the change process.

When this responsibility has been given, the remainder of the advisory service can play a very important but supplementary role in keeping the initiative in high profile. They can do this fairly easily by asking appropriate supportive questions when visiting a school. This need take up very little of their time but will show that it is an important initiative in their eyes. In addition they can, when planning their own subject-specific INSET for teachers, offer some training which will support the development of the whole school approach. All of this, of course, implies that they, like headteachers, need to be given a full understanding of the process of the course.

Finally, if the initiative is to have real credibility, an evaluation of the outcomes in schools will need to be built into the planning. If schools *know* that this will take place then, whatever other pressures occur, the initiative will remain in high profile and developments will take place. In teachers' eyes, if something is not worthy of being evaluated, then it cannot be very important.

This external evaluation need not be a large scale undertaking by the LEA but could take the form of monitoring school-identified targets as performance indicators at the appropriate times. The identification of these targets and agreed timing could very easily be built into the planning phase of the course. (Evaluation at the school level is included in the section below). The monitoring of negotiated targets in this way may not appear to offer an in-depth evaluation but it will exert a positive influence on the success of the implementation phase and will highlight issues and problems when the success or failure in achieving the targets is discussed.

At the school level

The head must select the link teachers with great care and, having done so, identify with them and senior management the strategy for the cascade process, including the identification of INSET time through GRIST, 'Baker Days' or directed time. The stages by which the school will move towards achieving its aims for special needs provision should be identified so that these stages can form the basis of the attainment targets within agreed time phases. The strategy should be explained to the whole staff well in advance and the purpose of it must be made clear. The link teachers can then negotiate targets and timings with individual departments, or even individual teachers, as appropriate, and can monitor these at the agreed times. This forward planning and monitoring of targets will ensure that the head's commitment is seen by all and will help all staff to feel some 'ownership' of their part in the developments which will, in turn, assist in keeping the initiative in high profile.

The head must also ensure that time is made available for the 'cascaders' to do their job effectively and for discussion at management level of any major structural changes which may be needed. If this kind of high profile planning is undertaken in advance and built into the school calendar, it will have more chance of keeping up the momentum for change even though the head may have to devote his or her attention to other issues once the cascade process has begun.

These, then, are some of the lessons learned from this pilot INSET project in special educational needs. They have helped to inform further presentations of the course to encourage a whole school approach to special needs in secondary schools within this LEA. In many ways, they have now become even more important because the 1988 Education Reform Act and the need to implement the National Curriculum and attainment testing are placing increasing demands on the limited time available to schools for in-service training.

It would not be appropriate here to discuss the many problems and uncertainties which now surround the education of students with special needs but it is clear that, in this context, INSET time for courses such as this could easily be crowded out by demands for training related to the new Act and issues such as the improvement of access to the whole curriculum for special needs students given low priority. One way forward might be to recognise the natural relationship which exists between the need to deliver the curriculum in appropriately differentiated forms, as anticipated by the National Curriculum, and the philosophy of the whole school approach to special needs. INSET could then be coordinated and integrated at the school level to meet the needs of both and to the ultimate benefit of the students. This should be the principal outcome of all in-service education.

[This article was first published in *British Journal of Special Education* Vol. 16, No. 1: March 1989.]

References

Arthur, H. (1988) *Special Needs: A Whole School Approach*. An appraisal of a course presented to Bedfordshire teachers 1986–87. Bedfordshire LEA.

Fullan, M. (1981) *Curriculum Implementation: A Resource Book*. Ontario: Ministry of Education.

Fullan, M. (1982) *The Meaning of Educational Change*. New York: Teachers College Press.

Fullan, M. (1985) 'Change Processes and Strategies at the Local Level'. *The Elementary School Journal*, **85**, 5.

Hopkins, D. (1986) 'The Change Process and Leadership in Schools'. *School Organisation*, **6**, 1.

Joyce B. and Showers, B. (1980) 'Improving Inservice Training: The Messages from Research'. *Education Leadership*, **37**: 379–385.

Rudduck, J. (1981) *Making the Most of the Short Inservice Course*. London: Schools Council, Working Paper 71.

CHAPTER 17

Concluding Remarks

Mel Ainscow and Anton Florek

The chapters in this book focus on three themes: the development of school policies, special educational needs in the classroom and staff development. Together these headings provide a useful agenda for groups of teachers wishing to review the policies of their schools with regard to special educational needs.

Within the context of such a review the content of the chapters provides a rich source of ideas. However, they do not represent a blueprint. They do not provide a set of easy instructions that can be followed in order to develop a whole school approach.

On the other hand they *are* a source of optimism and inspiration. The accounts of practice, the processes described and the ideas presented indicate the progress that has been made in many primary and secondary schools during recent years. It is on the basis of achievements such as these that those of us involved in the school system should look to the future.

What then of the future? How might we proceed towards this idea of a whole school approach to special educational needs? Any consideration of these questions must take account of the radical changes that are taking place in the education service, particularly those related to the Education Reform Act, 1988.

In this final chapter we consider some of the implications of these changes for the future development of special needs policies in ordinary schools. Our concern is with the combined effects of the following developments:

(1) National Curriculum and assessment
(2) Open enrolment to schools
(3) Grant-maintained schools
(4) Delegation of financial responsibilities from local authorities to their schools.

These major elements of Government policy, alongside the moves to introduce teacher appraisal, records of achievement and new arrangements for the funding of higher education, have major implications for the ways in which special educational needs are defined. They must also influence the ways in which schools respond to such needs.

In making comment on these developments we will try to provide a 'balance sheet'. On the credit side we present the potential advantages of the Education Reform Act; on the debit side we will examine some possible difficulties.

Possible advantages of recent policy changes

The initial reactions of many teachers to the proposals that are now incorporated in the 1988 Act tended to be negative. As the policies have taken shape, however, the profession seems to have become more open-minded. There appears to be a growing feeling that some of the policies, at least, may lead to improvements in schools.

In terms of policies for meeting special educational needs in ordinary schools five areas of possible advantage emerge. They are as follows:

Curriculum entitlement

Under the legislation all pupils share the same statutory entitlement to a broad and balanced curriculum, including access to the National Curriculum. This is surely a major step forward in promoting equal opportunity. In that sense it is consistent with all the material in this book with its emphasis on finding ways of making the curriculum in primary and secondary schools accessible to all pupils.

In the future, therefore, the aspiration of curriculum entitlement is one that becomes a legal requirement. For the special needs field this should signal the end of restricted opportunity for pupils perceived as having learning difficulties. Indeed it should provide further impetus to the development of whole school approaches.

Consistency

In a more practical sense the National Curriculum framework, with its attainment targets, programmes of study and arrangements for assessment, could provide other advantages to children who find learning difficult. Evidence from a range of research studies indicates that lack of consistency between teachers, and as pupils move from school to school, is likely to foster educational difficulties (e.g. Delamont and Galton, 1986; Mortimore *et al*, 1988). Greater agreement about purpose within the curriculum, including guidelines for progression, should help teachers to achieve a higher level of consistency within their work. It should also mean that difficulties arising from change of school can be reduced.

Assessment

The introduction of new forms of assessment based upon the recommendations of Professor Paul Black and his Task Group on Assessment and Testing (TGAT) may also have beneficial effects on practice. The issue of assessment is a matter of anxiety in many schools and some teachers find it a difficult and confusing topic.

The TGAT Report makes suggestions that are based upon good practice and modern thinking about assessment. In particular they emphasise the following features that are of benefit:

- providing teachers with information that can be used in deciding how a pupil's learning should be taken forward
- recording positive achievement with respect to what each pupil knows, understands and can do
- evaluating the effectiveness of the curriculum of schools in order that further efforts, resources or changes in practice might be introduced
- providing specific information for parents about the progress of their child, and general information to the community about the achievements of a school
- facilitating professional development as a result of teachers reflecting on their own practice and evaluating the outcome of their work.

The importance that is placed on assessing the progress of children through observation within the classroom must surely be of benefit in encouraging teachers to be more sensitive to the needs of individuals.

Funding flexibility

The moves towards delegation of responsibility for budget control to secondary schools and larger primary schools could (and should) provide advantages in those schools wishing to develop whole school policies. Elsewhere in this book the importance of resources is emphasised. The flexibility to redeploy resources within a school should be more feasible under the new arrangements. This assumes, of course, that appropriate policies are determined and successful management strategies adopted.

The key resource that will need to be considered is the staff. Head-teachers will have to consider within their budget how far staffing can be utilised to support individual teachers and particular departments as they attempt to develop new curriculum responses. This could give major encouragement to such initiatives and, at the same time, facilitate staff development.

Initial training

At conferences about special educational needs it is not uncommon to hear speakers and delegates argue that this topic needs far greater attention during initial teacher training. This is a fair point but one that should not be interpreted narrowly. If if were to lead to distinct elements within teacher training courses that emphasise separate responses to sub-groups of children perceived as being special, this would run counter to the trends that are current in schools.

What is needed is a greater emphasis on finding effective strategies for taking account of individual differences within the curriculum. In this respect the introduction of the National Curriculum and associated forms of assessment should help. It should mean that in future initial training courses will have a more specific agenda. Student teachers can be helped to consider how individual needs might be accommodated within a curriculum framework that is common to all schools. Consequently, courses should be more focused and new teachers better prepared in terms of what is expected of them.

Possible difficulties

Having considered some of the possible advantages of the recent legis-lation we need to look at the likely difficulties. In particular, what are the factors that may inhibit the further development of whole school approaches to meeting special educational needs? Once again five are potentially significant. They are:

Reductions in curriculum flexibility

We have already argued that the statement of curriculum entitlement for all pupils is a major step forward. It is important to remember, however, that a curriculum exists at a number of levels. For example the curriculum as stated may be different from the curriculum as practised. In terms of what is now being proposed our concern is that the National Curriculum, despite good intentions, may lead to classroom practice that is less responsive to the needs of individuals.

This reduction in flexibility may arise as a result of a number of interrelated factors. It may be, for example, that in some schools the introduction of the attainment targets, programmes of study and standard assessment tasks will lead to a narrowing of the curriculum focus. An emphasis on the achievement of narrowly conceived academic outcomes might then occur. Such a perspective would be to the disadvantage of those pupils whose progress was relatively slow.

Similarly, difficulties may occur if the curriculum is imposed with little attention given to the previous experience and personal interests of pupils, particularly those who come from homes where there are unusual cultural traditions. In this case some children may become alienated by their schooling and, as a result, less likely to give of their best efforts.

Exclusion

The notion of curriculum entitlement is also threatened by the various possibilities that exist for exclusion. In fairness it is important to recognise that emphasis is placed on dealing with special educational needs within the National Curriculum. The Department of Education and Science has argued that virtually all pupils will be able to record some progress through the ten levels of attainment to be covered during the period of compulsory education.

Nevertheless a range of procedures exists to modify or disapply National Curriculum requirements. Perhaps the most worrying of these is that relating to the writing of statements of special educational needs. Under the 1981 Education Act the purpose of a statement was to provide additional resources that might enable an individual to have access to the normal curriculum. As a result of the 1988 Act a statement can now be used as a means of excluding pupils from all or part of the National Curriculum. In other words the statement becomes a certificate of exclusion.

In the light of these arguments there is a need for vigilance to ensure that schools do not exclude larger numbers of pupils from the National Curriculum or the school in order to give a better impression of their aggregate performance on assessments at the reporting ages 7, 11, 14 and 16.

Streaming

Whilst the aim of helping pupils to work at their own levels of achievement is a sound one, the proposals for assessment may lead to another worrying possibility. The pressure to push some children along the ten levels of attainment may encourage some schools to re-introduce streaming systems. Indeed the idea of grouping by attainment rather than chronological age is already being contemplated in some schools.

If the outcome of all of this is the establishment of 'sink groups', with children feeling that nothing is expected of them, we will rapidly see a return to the worse features of pre-Warnock practice. This in turn will mean that the Government's aim of 'consistently high standards' will be unachievable.

Low achieving schools

A similar problem may emerge as a result of the Government's policy of using market forces to raise educational standards. This could lead to the development of 'sink schools'.

Where a particular school becomes unpopular in its local community, perhaps as a result of the publication of its assessment results, an inevitable spiral of deterioration may occur. Parents moving their children to other schools would lead to reductions in the budget which, in turn, could further reduce the achievements of the school.

Out of such a sad scenario it is possible to foresee situations where schools create special educational needs. A school in which there are insufficient staff, poor material resources, low morale and limited expectations is surely likely to mean that its pupils are likely to be less successful.

Reductions in support

A fifth difficulty that may well occur as a result of a combination of factors within the legislation relates to support for schools. Recent years have seen considerable progress in many local authorities towards the idea of an integrated special needs support service. Teams of advisers, advisory teachers and educational psychologists attempt to provide a coordinated range of advice and support. Increasingly the emphasis of this work is on assisting schools in their attempts to develop whole school approaches to special educational needs.

Under local management arrangements much of the budget for these services, currently controlled by local authorities, may be delegated to schools. Consequently headteachers will face difficult budgeting decisions. In the light of pressures for resources from various sources within their schools the allocation of funds to pay for advisory teacher input may become a low priority. Furthermore what money is available may be used to deal with individual children perceived as being problems rather than as a means of facilitating school-wide initiatives.

It should be added that where a whole school approach to meeting special educational needs is successful the need for outside support is reduced. This adds to the dilemma of headteachers as they attempt to balance their budgets. Should all available resources be concentrated on the development of in-house support networks? Or is it worthwhile paying for the services of external consultants? Difficult decisions indeed.

Conclusion

The aim of this final chapter has been to draw attention to the possible implications of recent Government policies for the further development of whole school approaches for special educational needs. Clearly it would be naive to read this book without reference to these trends.

In considering them, however, we have no need for despondency. The credit side of the balance sheet we have presented provides a range of potential benefits. If the difficulties noted on the debit side are minimised, the excellent practice described in the chapters of this book will provide a sound foundation for further progress in the future.

References

Delamont, S. and Galton, M. (1986) *Inside the Secondary Classroom.* London: Routledge and Kegan Paul.

Mortimore, P., Sammons, P., Stoll, L., Lewis, D and Ecob, R. *School Matters – The Junior Years.* Wells: Open Books.